Mirror Image
Breaking free from false reflections

Centre for
Faith and Spirituality
Loughborough University

PRESENCE BOOKS

Paris

Biblical quotations, unless otherwise noted are from the
New International Version © 1973, 1978, 1984 by the
International Bible Society.

ISBN 978-1-907228-27-8

Published by
PRESENCE BOOKS
on behalf of
MERCY MINISTRIES UK

Endorsements

This book completely reflects the heart of Mercy Ministries - its message of transformation through the Word of God is at the very core of the Mercy programme. Throughout the pages of this book Arianna's down to earth writing style teaches the reader the simple, practical steps of applying the Word of God so that it effects permanent change in our hearts and lives.

Nancy Alcorn, Founder and President, Mercy Ministries International

Poor self-image, and all its horrible consequences, is epidemic among women today and this book should be in every woman's handbag! There is so much good sense as well as God sense here. It's full of stories of the gloriously restored lives of countless broken young women who have found joy, hope and fulfillment in Jesus through the ministry of Mercy Ministries UK and Arianna Walker's leadership. I don't know anyone more qualified than Arianna to write this book; read it for yourself; and give it to your daughters, sisters and girlfriends and it will impact them for life!

Anne Coles – New Wine

Mirror Image has been written for all those who find themselves imprisoned by fears, doubts and insecurities. Arianna writes each chapter with a heart that wants to embrace, encourage, inspire and celebrate the real you that God sees. This book will give you a true reflection of your real beauty and value. Be free!

Charlotte Gambill- Abundant Life Church, Bradford

Mirror Image is a book that women of all ages can identify with. It deals with how we view ourselves outwardly and inwardly and unravels the issues and life experiences that can sometimes give us a distorted image. It is written in such a readable way and yet is a powerful tool. It will encourage you to take a deep look within and identify any issue God wants to lovingly work on in His beautifying process. I thoroughly endorse this book for personal reading and as a study guide with other women.

Marilyn Glass – Elim Pentecostal Church

Dedication

This book is dedicated to every woman who thinks that she is less than she is; every woman who feels lost, broken and beyond reach of the Father's love. May the pages of this book help you to know that God sees you; that he has plans to prosper you and not to harm you, plans to give you a hope and a future.

6   Mirror Image

With thanks

Thank you to every Mercy Ministries graduate whose stories fill the pages of this book with the power of transformed lives - you are my heroes.

Thank you to Nancy Alcorn whose incredible leadership, vision and faith-filled determination has been and will continue to be an incredible source of inspiration to me. You are a true hero of the faith and it is an honour to serve you.

Thank you to my amazing team - the women who day after day labour alongside me to build Mercy Ministries UK and increase its reach so that more young women can live a life of freedom and hope through a relationship with Jesus. You are all reflections of Him - you have become the mirror.

Thank you to my armour bearers - you know who you are. The times when your arms have held mine up are countless and I am so very grateful that we get to live this adventure together.

Thank you to my soul mate, my best friend, my amazing husband - you make my heart sing. You have played no small part in helping me find me in the face of distorted mirror images - thank you for always keeping it simple!

Thank you to two wonderful sons whose arrival in my life ignited a love like no other. You are amazing young men who are beginning to notice the false reflections around you, and I am so pleased that you see through the lies and believe the truth about who you are created to be. Keep going strong!

Thanks to those who helped make this book a reality - the proof reading, editing, constructive criticism and eye to detail has made all the difference.

And finally to my Father - words are not enough and so instead I will live from a grateful heart all the days of my life to bring glory to your Name.

All proceeds from the sale of this book go towards the work of Mercy Ministries UK.

Contents

10   Mirror Image

Foreword

Sometimes it seems that words are so inadequate to express the fullness of joy that comes in a dream being fulfilled. In making that statement, I am referring to the joy of seeing the first Mercy Ministries home in the UK flourish and thrive over the past 5 years, with many young women from all over Great Britain and Europe having an opportunity to experience God's unconditional love, forgiveness and life transforming power in partnership with local churches.

Although the vision of Mercy Ministries began in 1983, the dream to start a Mercy Ministries in the UK was birthed in the heart of Pastors Paul and Glenda Scanlon in July 1999 when we met for the first time - a divine connection that has led to growth on many levels.

The first UK Mercy home opened in 2006 as a result of that partnership and now 5 years later, I am so excited to be celebrating the opening of the new extension at MMUK. This extension enables the UK team to more than double the number of beds from 10 to 22 completely debt free- what a great testimony of God's grace and favour!"

This book is also a result of God's grace and favour; it completely reflects the heart of Mercy Ministries - its message of transformation through the Word of God is at the very core of the Mercy programme. Throughout the pages of this book Arianna's down to earth writing style teaches the reader the simple, practical steps of applying the Word of God so that it effects change in our hearts and lives.

'Mirror Image' reveals not only some of Arianna's own journey but it incorporates the stories of many young women who have had the opportunity to experience God's unconditional love, forgiveness and life transforming power. The power of this book lies in its simplicity - it's not complex in its message nor is it difficult to apply. The principles are built on the Word and through the sharing of personal experience, anecdotes and testimonies, the pages of this book have the power to transform.

My hope is that every woman who feels she is unworthy, not good enough, believing lies about her past, her present and her future, reads this book and connects with the heart of God towards her. My prayer is that hearts will be touched and minds will be renewed so that more women can experience the joy of wholeness and the power to reach others that comes from a transformed life.

Nancy Alcorn
Founder and President
Mercy Ministries International

Preface

Tell Her She is Looking in the Wrong Mirror

She was 17 years old, naturally blond and striking to look at. Tears streamed down her face as she lifted her eyes to meet mine. "I have an eating disorder," she whispered, barely audible.

I touched her arm and asked her how long she had been suffering for. She shrugged, "Years, on and off. I look in the mirror and I hate what I see." Taken aback, I asked her what she saw when she looked in the mirror. Her reply has haunted me ever since, "I look in the mirror and see a fat, ugly girl who is worthless and deserves to die."

It was then that I heard the Holy Spirit whisper, 'Tell her she is looking in the wrong mirror. Tell her that she is believing a false reflection and that I will show her a true reflection, if she chooses to look.' That was five years ago and since then, as part of my role at Mercy Ministries, I have met many more girls like her.

Mercy Ministries was founded in the U.S.A. in 1983 by Nancy Alcorn. After many years of working in women's prisons and in social services, she realised that without a Christ-centred approach, the cycle of destruction in the lives of those around her would continue.

Now, 28 years later, Mercy Ministries runs homes across the world, offering a 6 month residential programme that transforms the lives of young women between the ages of 18 and 28, who face life-controlling issues such as depression, eating disorders, self-harm and the emotional effects of abuse. The Mercy Ministries programme is voluntary, Christ-centered and completely free of charge. It has been my honour and privilege to be part of developing this great ministry in the UK.

MMUK opened its doors to young women on September 4th, 2006 and since then, we have seen God reveal to girl after girl the power that comes from believing truth over lies; the freedom that comes with putting that truth into action and the beauty of a true reflection in the mirror of God's word.

To this day, that first girl I met years before we opened the doors of MMUK still haunts me. I wonder where she is, what she is doing and if she ever pulled through.

I don't even know her name, yet she had a lasting impact on me and set me on a journey that now has me sitting at a desk writing a book which began with that conversation. If you're out there, I hope you get to read this one day.

Arianna Walker
June 2011

Introduction

Forgetting What We Look Like

It's a rainy Friday afternoon; the Mercy residents are all out on their weekly shopping trip and after a challenging week in the office, one of the staff has decided it's time for some comic relief. So here we are, laughing our heads off; some of us have tears smudging our mascara as we look at the hilarious distortions the Apple Mac 'Photo Booth' application is showing us.

The 'photo booth' is basically a camera on the screen that takes your picture and then distorts it to epically hilarious proportions; and it really is the thing to do whenever someone needs to see the funny side of life!

It's a bit like the 21st century, hi-tech version of the old hall of mirrors you used to get at fairgrounds. The kind that make you look like you have a head the size of a pea and a body that could give Frankenstein's monster a run for his money. Each reflection shows you a distortion of your true self and the absurdity of the reflection is hilarious.

Life can be like one of those hall of mirrors (or Photo Booth for those of you who speak Apple Mac). We are constantly bombarded with images and different mirrors that try to show us who we are, but the truth is that many of those images are tainted. They don't show our true reflection but we can fail to realise it and begin to believe the distorted image we are faced with.

Over time, these false images begin to affect everything we do - how we relate to others, the decisions we make, our thinking patterns, coping mechanisms and even the future we are believing for.

Soon after my conversation with that first heart-broken young girl, I turned to James 1[1] which says:

> *Do not merely listen to the word, and so deceive yourselves. Do what it says. Anyone who listens to the word but does not do what it says is like a man who looks at his face in a mirror and, after looking at himself, goes away and immediately forgets what he looks like. But the man who looks intently into the perfect law that gives freedom, and continues to do this, not forgetting what he has heard, but doing it - he will be blessed in what he does.*

It got me thinking about the amount of times I have looked in the mirror and hated what I saw; the times when I have forgotten who I am and what I believe about myself and about the one who made me.

James tells us that God's mirror leads to blessings and freedom. Therefore, it's safe to assume that these false mirrors will do the opposite; they will trap us, hold us captive and steal our blessing. They will make us forget what we look like.

I want to invite you to come on a journey with me. A journey that will uncover some of the false mirrors you may be looking in, and show you your true reflection in God's mirror.

Once we expose these 'false mirrors' in our lives it gives us the knowledge and therefore the power to make informed choices about which mirrors we look in.

---

[1] James 1:22 – 25 NIV version

So let me ask, what mirror are you looking in today? Do you see the real you, or is a false reflection staring back at you?

Many of these mirrors are ones that I have identified from my own journey and from working with women for many years now. I believe there are simple tools available to us that will enable us to break free from the false reflections and into a revelation of the true refection God's mirror presents to us.

My hope is that this book becomes a catalyst for permanent change in your life and that it sets you off on a journey of discovering the wonderful freedom that comes from knowing who you are.

Let me pray for you:

Holy Spirit, I ask that each reader who invests the time to read this book will be met by your presence. I pray that she will feel your gentle guidance as you bring her to revelation and truth about herself, her identity and her worth. I pray that Truth will enter her heart and mind and as it does so, that the Truth would set her free.

In Jesus' Name,
Amen.

18   Mirror Image

Chapter 1

Dare to Bare:
The Dressing Room Mirror

Imagine a dressing room mirror, surrounded by light bulbs. An actress is seated in front of it covering her face with a thick mask of make-up to help her adopt a new persona and deliver the star performance everyone expects.

Many of us do exactly the same every day. We put on a false mask and become who we need to be to give the pin-up performance expected of us. This is the 'dressing room mirror.' It represents the mirror of our fake identity, our carefully constructed cover-up.

Hannah, a Mercy Ministries UK graduate, writes;

> 'I came to Mercy Ministries expecting to be punished for who I was and for the things I'd done. I was living a very deceptive life, everything was hidden under a mask. But at Mercy, I was not judged. I was loved, accepted and given an amazing amount of grace. I learnt how to feel safe with people. I found an intimate relationship with God and eventually gave him my heart. I worked through the deep hurts and found true joy.
>
> Before I came to Mercy, I was hiding my issues behind masks. I was bulimic, I was depressed, I was suicidal, I was fearful, I was hopeless and I was a broken girl. But I came to Mercy Ministries and chose not to let those words define me. I chose life.

I let go of the past and I learnt how to forgive. I let go of my bad habits and coping mechanisms. I saw myself differently, as someone new. I knew I'd never be the same again.

Amy, another graduate, says it like this;

'The only way I could effectively release the pain was through cutting myself. I began to believe I was losing my mind as I chopped and changed from being content, to being depressed, from starvation to midnight binges, and from self-harming to suicidal fantasies. I hated life.

I hated myself. I recall standing on the edge of the cliff top near to where I live, tears streaming down my face, staring at the rocks below and believing that with one jump I could escape all of the pain.

At Mercy, God gently removed the masks that I constantly hid behind and he broke down the walls and barriers that I had built up to protect myself.'

I chose these two stories because both of them use these phrases, 'God removed the masks that I hid behind' and 'I was hiding my issues behind masks.'

Wearing masks, hiding behind a false identity, is a natural reaction to pain and is often used as a defence mechanism to express our hurt or to protect ourselves from more hurt. These behaviours become masks that cover our real identities.

If you look into a mirror while wearing a mask, the reflection does not show your true face. It is the same with the mirror of God's word, if we wear a mask, we hide ourselves from its truth. In order to see the truth that can set us free, we must remove every mask that prevents us from discovering our true reflection.

There used to be a TV programme called 'What not to Wear', which was presented by two women, Trinny and Susannah.

Each episode features a different woman who has hit rock bottom in her self-esteem for various reasons. She may have been through a recent divorce, suffer from depression or just simply hate herself. Each week the featured woman so lacked in confidence that she would hide herself away in baggy t-shirts and men's trousers.

If you've ever seen it you will know that these two women are ruthless. Instead of sitting this poor woman down to find out why she struggles with herself so much and offer empathic advice, they strip her down to her underwear and make her face herself in a three way mirror. This woman who was too ashamed of her appearance to stand in front of a full-length mirror now has her true reflection exposed for all to see. To top it off, they prod and poke all her wobbly bits on national TV!

I have no idea why anyone would volunteer for that kind of torture but actually when you watch it closely you see an amazing thing happen. Once the woman has got past the shock of seeing what she really looks like, she begins a journey of learning to love herself, wobbly bits and all.

Many times I've watched the programme and been impacted by the freedom that can come simply from having the guts to strip off and face reality; to come from behind the baggy clothes and face what really lies beneath. Facing reality and having the guts to face facts; to look at ourselves and be real about what we see, is a very powerful tool to use when overcoming the falseness of the 'dressing room mirror'.

Hiding ourselves is a natural human reaction to guilt, shame and pain. In Genesis 3:8[2] we see Adam and Eve's immediate reaction to their choice to disobey God. It says:

> *At that moment their eyes were opened, and they suddenly felt shame at their nakedness. So they sewed fig leaves together to cover themselves. When the cool evening breezes were blowing, the man and his wife heard the Lord God walking about in the garden. So they hid from the Lord God among the trees. Then the Lord God called to the man, "Where are you?" He replied, "I heard you walking in the garden, so I hid. I was afraid because I was naked."*

Adam and Eve hid from God because of their guilt and shame. God asked them where they were, not because he didn't know, but because he can only begin to work with us when we are prepared to step out and reveal exactly where we are.

When you are lost and call someone for directions, the very first question they will ask is 'where are you?' In order for us to receive direction and input from God, he needs to know that we are prepared to accurately describe our present location, no matter how far from the right track it may appear to be.

When Adam and Eve hid, covering themselves with leaves, they effectively found themselves before a 'dressing room mirror.' It's as if they painted on fake smiles, covering over the blemishes and ugly pimples on their lives that they were suddenly so aware and ashamed of.

It's interesting to note that Adam and Eve covered their most intimate parts with leaves. We all do the same when we hide from God; we hide our most intimate parts and fear

---

[2] Genesis 3:8 -10 NIV version

him seeing us naked. But God created us to be revealed before him, because in him we have nothing to be ashamed of.

There is often a cycle of shame, fear and control at work that causes us to want to hide. We can see that in the scripture when Adam said: 'I was afraid because I was naked, so I hid myself.' We might recognise it as: I am afraid that you will find out about the real me, how dysfunctional I really am, how ashamed I am, so I will control how close you get to me, or I will control what part of me you see.

If we want freedom and wholeness we must be prepared to lay ourselves bare before God. Shame, fear, and control are primary forces that work against us and will try to stop us from trusting God and so damage our intimacy and walk with him.

King David understood this when he wrote Psalm 139[3] :

> God, investigate my life; get all the facts firsthand. I'm an open book to you; even from a distance, you know what I'm thinking. You know when I leave and when I get back; I'm never out of your sight. You know everything I'm going to say before I start the first sentence. I look behind me and you're there, then up ahead and you're there, too - your reassuring presence, coming and going. This is too much, too wonderful - I can't take it all in!'
>
> 'Investigate my life, O God, find out everything about me; Cross-examine and test me, get a clear picture of what I'm about; See for yourself whether I've done anything wrong - then guide me on the road to eternal life.

David dared to bare himself before God, not because he thought he was perfect but because he understood that in

---

[3] Psalm 139; The Message

order for God to do his work he had to invite God in and give him an 'access-all- areas' pass.

2 Corinthians 3:18[4] says; 'So our faces are not covered. They show the bright glory of the Lord, as the Lord's Spirit makes us more and more like our glorious Lord.'

Is your face uncovered? Are you allowing God access to make you more and more like him, or do you sit at the dressing room mirror carefully applying your mask to present to the world a star performance?

So now, let's identify a few of the masks by name. Some are masks we deal with on a regular basis with the girls we support in Mercy, and others are masks that I have had to lay down in my own life.

The mask of perfectionism and performance

This mask sounds like: 'I must not show weakness, failure, struggle of any kind because I am a Christian, a leader, an example and I have to maintain the picture perfect image that people have of me.'

Or it may sound like: 'I have to earn love and respect, so I will perform and become all that is expected of me, never showing anyone my weaknesses. Yet I know that I am weak and therefore doomed to failure, so I must try harder, be better and keep improving myself.'

In other words, doing good equals being good. This is a false identity, a mask that will stop God being able to get close. Not only that, but people will struggle to get close too. It's actually pride to think that we can be even anywhere near perfect this side of heaven, or to think that we can impress God with our goodness, our works, our ability to perfect ourselves, or our success.

---

[4] 2 Cor 3:18; The Message

The fact is none of us are perfect no matter how hard we try. God is not a strict teacher who points out our faults, so we can go and fix ourselves and then present ourselves to him for the next fault to be worked on. God sees past our imperfections and our failings and in his love chooses to use our lives for great things anyway. When you look at many of the characters in the Bible who achieved great things, they were definitely far from perfect.

The Apostle Paul was someone who understood weakness. In 2 Corinthians he mentions a 'tormentor', a thorn in his flesh that he asked God to remove three times. He records God's answer in 2 Corinthians 12:9[5];

> *'Each time he said, "My grace is all you need. My power works best in weakness." So now I am glad to boast about my weaknesses, so that the power of Christ can work through me.'*

Paul understood that weakness isn't something to fear; we are simply not designed to live in our own strength. We don't need to strive for perfection because our weakness gives God the opportunity to demonstrate the fullness of his strength in our lives. Yes, work together with the Holy Spirit to grow and learn as a person but do not expect ever to reach perfection and don't beat yourself up when you fail.

The victim mask

The mask of the 'Victim' is another that we can allow to cover our lives. It sounds like this; 'Nothing ever works out for me; I always get disappointed; people will always let me down; I might as well not even try because I'll just get hurt.'

Victim mentality tells us that we have a right to be a

---

[5] 2 Cor 12:9 NIV

victim, that it's everyone else's fault and therefore we carry no responsibility towards our freedom.

Some don't want to remove the victim mask because without it there's no excuse for not trying, for not taking responsibility for their own choices, and for the path they choose to walk.

This mask protects against the fear of failure because a 'victim' thinks failure is all that can be expected from them. The victim mask makes us believe that there is no hope, there is no chance of living free and not even God can fix us, so what's the point of even trying?

A 'victim' believes their problems are a result of what has happened to them and no-one can change that. Not even God!

Some of us have lived with our conditions, issues and behaviours for so long that we develop an attachment to them. A 'victim' fears removing the mask. They don't know who they are without their issue or problem to define them.

A victim mentality asks, 'Will people still be my friend if I don't need them to pray for me, give support and rally round me all the time?

To be free from this mask we must be prepared to let go of the past, which is described in more detail later in this book.

The mask of inadequacy

Moses told God he couldn't speak, Gideon was convinced he was a weak man not the warrior God had called him, Saul hid in the baggage when he was meant to be anointed as King. All of these men who did incredible exploits for God at first hid behind the mask of inadequacy as a reason for God not to call upon them. The leaders God chose to spearhead some of his greatest moves, struggled with inadequacy.

Inadequacy is a mask many people wear, which keeps God from being able to use us. The fact is that we are small, we are inadequate and we will always be inadequate and unworthy for what God calls us to do. It is not *our* adequacy or worthiness that causes him to use us, it's *his* adequacy and *his* worthiness. We have to stop looking to ourselves, our own strength, our own abilities and instead look to his strength and grace that will work through us.

When he uses us for his purposes, it's never because of who we are and what we can do but who he is and what he can do through us. When we complain to God about our inadequacy, it only shows that we are looking to our own strength and not to his strength in us.

Taking off the mask of inadequacy means we look to God for what we do not have and recognise that God delights to show His power through the imperfect. In fact, it is our imperfections that create space for God's power to be manifest.

Did you know that what distinguishes a genuine pearl from a fake one is its imperfections? It's the irregular sphere, the faint sense of grit on the surface of the genuine pearl that sets it apart from the counterfeit smoothness of a fake one and it is by this imperfection that its value is found. In the same way, it's our imperfections that give us authenticity as a human being.

The mask of independence

'I must make it on my own; people have left me, hurt me, abandoned me, God has disappointed me, so I will do this thing called life alone, without anyone's help. You can't count on anyone but yourself,' so speaks independence.

This mask will allow you to control how close people get to you by making you believe that no one can ultimately be trusted and therefore you must protect yourself. People do this by building up an internal barrier, but although it succeeds in keeping people out, it has the unfortunate side effect of keeping you locked behind it, isolated and alone. Independence does not like to show vulnerability or need and so this mask will cause you to suffer alone, silent behind a self made wall of growing anger and frustration yet not being prepared to reach out for help.

The mask of sarcasm, bitterness, criticism and blame.

This mask will use any of the above to put others down (in the case of sarcasm, we can put others down *and* get a laugh!), but the underlying motivation is to make us feel better about ourselves. We find fault with others to reconcile the faults in ourselves that we are desperately trying to hide. This mask acts like a reflective shield, cleverly and tactically defending your self esteem and value by the tearing down of others.

The mask of a lively personality

Clearly, some people genuinely have a lively, life and soul of the party personality type; it is not a mask to them. On the other hand, there are those who wear this personality like a mask, aware that their smile hides the pain inside.

I once watched an interview with the singer Robbie Williams. He had just performed an incredible show to over 80,000 people. Alone on the stage, he held their attention by performing some of his best hits in addition to laughing, joking and being all they wanted him to be. "Let me entertain you" he sang and the crowd cheered him on.

But after the show was over, he sat in front of the camera and revealed a rare look behind the mask. Asked by the interviewer whether he enjoyed the show, he shrugged and said that it was just a show.

His eyes revealed a sad discontent, as he said it was a personality he put on to be able to do what he does, but underneath it all he would swap it in a heartbeat to find happiness, peace and contentment. He admitted he wore a mask, a fake smile to hide the pain.

The mask of passivity

This mask will make you feel safe by doing nothing. It's the same defence mechanism many animals use; the ostrich buries her head in the sand in the hope that the threat will leave; the opossum plays dead for the same reason and the potato beetle larva simply covers itself in its own toxic excrement to create a stench so bad nothing will come close!

Doing nothing means you at least can't be blamed for failing. If you never try to build close relationships, you can't be rejected; if you don't take the test, you can't fail it; if you don't expect anything, you won't be disappointed.

If you never even try, then you will not have to face the pain of knowing that your effort wasn't good enough. This mask will lead you to live your life as a passive bystander, watching the world go by whilst you find a level of comfort in the smallness of your world because there is at least no risk attached.

The mask of "I'm too busy"

This mask is too busy to face up to itself; too busy doing things for God, for other people. The bonus of this mask is that we don't even have to feel guilty about not facing ourselves, God, or anyone else because busyness means at least we are getting things done! We hide from what matters by filling our time with what doesn't, yet we convince ourselves that all this busyness is legitimate, necessary and therefore justified.

If the motivation behind your busyness is to keep the attention off yourself and distract you from facing the issues you need to address, then it is a mask.

Revelation is not transformation

You may have read through the list of masks and had a revelation that one (or more) of them applies to you. That's great and it's good, but it mustn't end there. Having a revelation about something means that a truth has been revealed to you. But something has to be done about it in order for that revelation to become transformation in your life. The next step is crucial in the process… you have to peel off the mask and dare to bare all.

Queen Esther wore a mask for many years. Her true identity as a poor, orphaned Jewish girl was hidden from those around her and for a season, this false identity protected her and kept her safe.

There may be times in our lives when God will allow us to wear our masks for a season; a time where we choose to hide ourselves like Esther did.

Yet, there came a time in Esther's life where she was presented with a choice. This was no longer just about her life: the King, her husband, was going to give a command for her own people, the Jews to be killed. The lives of thousands of people depended on her being brave enough to take off the mask and reveal her true identity to those around her. Would she have the courage to do it? Could she dare to bare?

Esther's first reaction was fear - she could be killed if she approached the King uninvited, especially to tell him that she is in fact, one of the people he has sentenced to death.

But her uncle Mordecai says this in reply to her fears:

'When Esther's words were reported to Mordecai, he sent back this answer: "Do not think that because you are in the king's house you alone of all the Jews will escape. For if you remain silent at this time, relief and deliverance for the Jews will arise from another place, but you and your father's family will perish. And who knows but that you have come to royal position for such a time as this?"[6]

God is calling time on the masks that you are hiding behind. Will you have the courage to peel them off, to be real and transparent? There are people who need you to be who you are called to be.

They need you to step into your true identity in Christ, so that you can lead them to safety. There are many people who will be reached by your courage to strip the masks off your life, just as in Esther's life.

Like Esther, you have a choice, but remember Mordecai's words because they are written for us all to read. God will surely reach those who you are meant to reach in some other way. He will accomplish all that he has purposed in his people's lives with or without you. But the effects of not removing the masks will affect firstly your own life and then those whose lives you have a direct impact on; your husband, children, family and friends.

Taking off a mask, a false identity, can feel a little like having surgery. When I gave birth to my children, I had to have surgery to get them out. I've had two caesarean sections, so I know from personal experience how painful and frightening surgery can be. But in the end, being cut and my flesh being exposed (with no clothes allowed to cover up and hide behind during surgery!) brought forth new life. Going through that painful process brought a new beginning

---

[6] Esther 4: 12 -14 NIV version

to my life; it released a whole new expression of a part of me that had not been seen before… motherhood.

In the same way that we experience surgery physically, we can experience surgery at an emotional and spiritual level. God is a master surgeon and he specializes in internal heart surgery. He is the expert, and yes, it can be painful and frightening but it is part of the process.

I believe that allowing him access to all the areas of our hearts and choosing to remove the mask so he can get close enough, will mean new life; a new season and a whole new expression of a part of you waiting for its moment to shine.

So let me ask, are you wearing masks, if so what are they and are you prepared to remove them? Are you ready to look into the mirror of God's word without the layers of self-protection?

If so, then let's do something about it! Find some paper and write down what masks you have identified. Commit yourself to God anew, then rip up the paper and throw it in the bin.

Let's be clear, this is not for any other reason than it's sometimes a good idea to make your body follow through with a decision your spirit has already made. Writing your mask down on a piece of paper and throwing it in the bin has no power whatsoever. The power is in the decision you are making to come from behind your mask and dare to look into the mirror of God's word barefaced, trusting him with the rest.

The lyrics from Natalie Grant's song 'Real Me' beautifully describe the process of removing a mask and becoming comfortable with what's underneath.

Real Me

Foolish heart looks like we're here again
Same old game of plastic smile
Don't let anybody in
Hiding my heartache
Will this glass house break?

How much will they take
Before I'm empty
Do I let it show?
Does anybody know?

Chorus:
But You see the real me
Hiding in my skin
Broken from within
Unveil me completely
I'm loosening my grasp
There's no need to mask my frailty
Oh, Cause You see the real me

Painted on
Life is behind a mask
Self-inflicted circus clown
I'm tired of the song and dance
Living a charade
Always on parade
What a mess I've made of my existence
But You love me even now
And still I see somehow

Oh, Cause You see the real me

Bridge:
Wonderful, beautiful
Is what You see
When You look at me
You're turning the tattered fabric of my life into
A perfect tapestry

Oh, I just wanna be me
I wanna be me
Chorus
Cause You see the real me
Wonderful, beautiful
Is what You see
When You look at me

Set aside time today, tomorrow or whenever you get the opportunity, and have a conversation with God about the 'dressing room mirror' in your life. My prayer is that you will have the courage to come from behind whatever you thought was protecting you and allow God to reveal the real you.

Summary: How to break free from the Dressing Room Mirror:

1. Remember that freedom and wholeness will only ever be yours if you are prepared to lay yourself bare before God.

2. Make a decision to bare your 'nakedness' in the mirror before God, of all the false masks you are hiding behind.

3. Identify the mask(s) you are hiding behind e.g. Perfectionist, Victim, Inadequacy, Independence, Sarcasm, Bitterness, Criticism, Blame, Lively Personality, or Passivity

4. Ask God to reveal to you any additional mask(s) that you may not be aware of.

5. Write these down (it makes for a sobering reality in seeing them in your own handwriting!) so that you can hold yourself accountable to breaking free from them.

6. Work together in partnership with God to do the work of changing you on the inside. Don't try to be God and try to fix yourself, but hold His hand and allow Him to walk you through the process of changing your heart and mind on a daily basis, as you begin to change the way you approach your life and the people around you from a place of authenticity and not from a false identity.

Prayer

Thank you for revealing to me the masks that I have been hiding behind.

I don't want to live under a cycle of shame, fear and control any longer.

I now give you complete access to every part of my heart and mind; allowing you to heal me of any of the past hurts and disappointments that have caused me to put those masks on in the first place.

I thank you that you have already given me the victory and that you are strengthening me daily as I walk in the truth of everything your Word promises for my future.

Help me to not fall back into the trap of these masks when

challenges come my way, but to fix my eyes firmly on you, the Author and Perfecter of my faith, to show me who I am.

Lord, I thank you that with you all things are possible, that this is just the beginning, and that through ridding myself of every aspect of my identity that is not rooted in you, many more after me will be rescued also - family, friends, and those people you will connect me with who I don't even know yet.

Thank you for all you have already done and are about to do.

In Jesus' name,

Amen.

Chapter 2

Don't Look Back:
The Rear-View Mirror

Rear-view mirrors are essential when it comes to driving safely. We need to look behind us because it's important to understand and be aware of what's behind, in order to move forward safely.

Yet, if you were driving your car and were looking intently into the rear-view mirror for an extended period of time, sooner or later you would come to a standstill; either with a crash and a bang or because you'd become so engrossed with what was behind you, you'd have forgotten to keep your foot down.

When you look intently into the mirror of your past, your rear-view mirror, this is what you will see:

- your **failures**
- your **past hurts**
- your **regrets**

Pain, bitterness, unforgiveness and offense lurk in this mirror's reflection.

The words that still cut through your soul every time you think of them will come crashing back into view when you look in this mirror. Your reflection will become distorted by bitterness, unforgiveness and anger if you choose to spend any length of time gazing at this reflection.

The people who hurt you, the choices you made, the things you said and the things said to you, are all present in this reflection. Disappointment, pain and destruction are enhanced and magnified by this mirror. It has sharp edges that will reopen old wounds and you will be unable to see an image of yourself without those wounds.

We all have a past, we all have regrets and some of us have to deal with the painful consequences of things that have happened. But be warned, constantly looking behind will stop you moving forward safely.

Look ahead not behind

The fact is, gazing into the rear view mirror at the wrong moment can cause you to crash. Genesis 19 tells the story of Lot, his wife and their children. They lived in a place called Sodom, which God was going to destroy because of its wickedness. God told them to get out immediately or they would be swept away in the destruction of the city. Lot hesitated, so the angels that God had sent, took him by the hand and led them out of the city.

Once they reached safety, one of the angels warned them to run for their lives without looking back and not to stop anywhere on the plains. They were clearly warned they would be swept away if they stopped to gaze in their rearview mirror. God had prepared a safe place for them in the mountains, but despite this, Lot begged the angels to let him and his family stay closer to Sodom. So the angels let them take refuge in a small village nearby.

You would think that Lot and his wife would have been glad to leave the evil and wickedness of Sodom behind and step into the new future God had provided for them. But unfortunately Lot's wife hesitated; she disobeyed what the angels had said and looked back instead of focusing on what lay ahead. It was a costly mistake and she paid for that backwards glance into her rear-view mirror with her life.

When God says it's time to move on, you can become hesitant like Lot was. There is a grace and an understanding for this, as this story shows. God will take us by the hand and lead us just as the angel did with Lot.

He will lead us through the process of escaping our past and into a new future. For some, this journey will not be an easy one. It will require forgiveness, determination and wisdom from people you trust, but as long as you are moving forward and keeping your hand in his, he will, through his grace and mercy, still rescue us.

Sometimes, as part of dealing with our past, we have to go back in order to set things right. We might have to forgive those who hurt us, we might need counselling or mentoring to work through some of the issues from our past. That's okay for a season, but for everyone without exception, there will come a time when God draws a line and asks you to move on. To let it go and trust him with your future by letting go of your past.

Setting the pace

God wants to lead us on a journey which takes us from our past and into our future. He wants to get some momentum going in our lives to get us moving in the right direction; yet he allows us to set the pace. When Lot said that he wanted to flee to a village that was closer to Sodom, God allowed this. It wasn't God's first choice but he allowed Lot to take smaller steps to his freedom, as long as he did not stop moving and did not look back.

The same goes for us. Never be afraid that God will make you deal with your past at a rate you are not able to sustain. God can (and sometimes does) bring emotional healing in an instant but very often he will go at the pace we set. Sometimes we need to get counselling and talk through the painful issues from our past with a professional or someone we trust. Sometimes a person will need to find expert help such as the support we provide at Mercy Ministries but whatever the journey from your past into your future looks like, there is one common denominator for all. There will come a moment when God asks us to let go, to leave it all behind, to no longer identify with who we were, what we did, or what was done to us in the past. Instead we must embrace the amazing future he has planned through the power of forgiveness.

Lot's wife struggled to let go of the past. She probably had family, friends, a job; her whole life was in that place, but God called her out of it because there was no future for her there. Yet she did not trust him, she clung on to her past and it cost her everything - her hopes, her dreams, her potential, her chance of freedom and ultimately, her life.

When we decide to look in the rear-view mirror and allow the past to dominate our outlook, it can also cause the death of our hopes, dreams and potential.

Don't make the same mistake. Don't fear letting go of the past. Trust that God is taking you to a new future and will lead you to a place of safety.

God's mirror will release you into your future, not trap you in your past.

I remember as a child going to the circus and watching in awe as the trapeze artist moved with grace and courage through the air - to me it looked like she was flying. At just the right moment, seconds before gravity would demand its price, her hands grabbed the next trapeze and she would fly again.

I imagine the most frightening moment for the trapeze artist must be when she has to let go of the trapeze she is holding onto. The timing has to be perfect and she must not fear the moment where she is left empty handed; for without letting go of one, she cannot take hold of the other. It would be a poor show if all the crowd could see is a person clinging onto a trapeze for dear life, refusing to let go and so ending up swinging aimlessly back and forth until she gradually slows down to a stop.

Yet many of us live our lives like that. We swing back and forth giving the impression to all who watch that there is in fact motion in our lives, when all the while, we are simply covering the same ground over and over again. We may not enjoy the experience, but we remain stuck in the same place because we refuse to let go and trust God to catch us.

The excitement, the adrenalin, the very purpose of being a trapeze artist is to fly, to soar, to feel the air all around and then to safely grab the trapeze that swings into your line of sight just in time to take you to the next one.

Moving forward will always require you to let go of the past and trust that God will help you grab what's coming with both hands. It's not enough to release just one hand from the bar. You can't hold on to your past and grasp your future at the same time. If you try to hold onto both trapezes, you will find yourself in conflict, under pressure, and left dangling in a very uncomfortable position.

God will always fill your empty space; he is drawn to it. The trouble is most of us are so full of the things we refuse to let go of, that there's no space left for God to fill.

We fear the emptiness of that space. We fear who we will be when the past no longer defines us. We don't trust God with our future and so we choose to look back and that mirror traps us again.

Jeremiah 29:11 says, "For I know the plans I have for you," says the Lord, "plans to prosper you and not to harm you, plans to give you hope and future." God has a future planned for us. It is a future where we have the strength to help others, where our issues are no longer holding us captive. But all the things we dream of, the plans we have, the longing for purpose, meaning and usefulness in our lives, will be ours only when we dare to let go of the things that are trapping us in our past.

Turning remorse into resolve

We have to decide that enough is enough and choose to stop sabotaging our future by gazing at the past. I call it 'turning remorse into resolve'.

In the Collins' English Dictionary the word 'remorse' means 'a sense of deep regret and guilt'. It comes from the Latin word 'remorsus' which means 'a gnawing inside.'

This is such an accurate description of the turmoil caused in our lives when we continue to gaze at a mirror image distorted by the past. It can create a gnawing sensation of being trapped by guilt, shame, fear, despair and hopelessness day after day.

But 'resolve' on the other hand, means this: 'to decide or determine firmly, to change, alter, to make up the mind of; cause or decide, to find the answer or solution, to bring to an end, a firmness of purpose and determination.'

To me 'resolve' describes what it looks like to take your eyes off the rear-view mirror and fix it firmly ahead. Having resolve will result in change, and give you a 'whatever it takes' attitude to being transformed and made whole; to be released from the trap of the past.

This changing remorse into resolve is something we have been privileged to witness in the lives of so many young women who have been through the Mercy Ministries' programme.

Kirsten, one of our beautiful graduates said,

> 'My life before Mercy Ministries is best described as
> hopeless; always striving for happiness and love,
> perfection and control, but never being able to attain
> any of it. I spent so much of my life trying to fix
> everything including myself, but the more I tried the
> more out of control everything got; till eventually I
> gave up trying. I allowed the depression and
> addictions that were controlling my life to overtake
> me.
>   Then I came to a point in my life where I had had
> enough. Mercy was literally my last hope. I knew that
> this had to work. I knew that things had to change;
> that I had to change. I had tried it every other way,
> now I had to try it God's way.'

That is what turning 'remorse' into 'resolve' looks like.
There is a reason why the rear-view mirror is so small, it's
only meant for the odd glance, to help you set your course
forward.

The key that unlocks the door

Sometimes we can feel trapped by our past. It's like being
locked in a room where the smallest thing can bring back a
memory that triggers feelings of anger, hurt, betrayal and
rejection, so we bang on the door screaming to be let out.
We get angry at the people who put us in that room and we
demand to be let out. But, although we don't realise it all
along we have the key in our own hands.

The key that can unlock the prison of your past and set
you free is forgiveness. Without forgiveness, true freedom is
impossible. Without forgiveness, we will remain locked in
that room.

Unless you learn to forgive, the door to your future will stay firmly locked and you will remain a prisoner of your past. These are strong words but Jesus was very clear about the need for forgiveness. He said: 'But if you do not forgive men their sins, your Father will not forgive your sins.'[7]

Forgiveness is a choice to begin a process that may take time. Forgiveness rarely comes from feelings, in fact our feelings will often work against us. It requires an act of your will, an act of obedience to God's will. Right feelings follow right actions and as you act on the decision to forgive, the feelings will eventually follow. If you ask him to help you I can guarantee you he will!

Perhaps you have been the victim of unspeakable pain, hurt, betrayal or abuse. Maybe you can't even remember a time when you haven't been mistreated or misunderstood in some way. These kinds of events can make us feel justified to live in unforgiveness. These things seem too painful to forgive; you feel that your resentment and hatred of the people that hurt you is deserved.

You may think, 'Surely if I forgive such devastating trespasses, it's like excusing them or accepting that what they did was okay?' But this isn't how forgiveness works. Forgiveness fully accepts and acknowledges the hurt and pain that has been caused. It does not belittle it, nor does it justify the behaviour of those who hurt you. Instead, it chooses to take the burden of judgement from your back and places it onto Jesus'.

Dead man walking

I once asked God to help me explain the damage unforgiveness can cause and he showed me a picture of a person walking along a road with a corpse on their back. It

---

[7] Matthew 6;15 NIV

was rotting with a foul stench and toxic fumes radiating from it. The person carrying the corpse was unaware of the smell, they couldn't see poison from the corpse seeping into the friction burns its weight had caused on their back. She walked along, burdened by the weight of her unforgiveness with anger propelling her forward and pain causing her to stumble every now and then.

Friends would walk alongside to try and tell the person about the corpse, but she didn't trust anyone enough to listen. Instead she would scowl to chase them off, or smile sweetly to make them think she had heard them while the corpse continued to infect her.

Then I saw God hand the person a huge pair of scissors with 'choose to forgive' written on them. As the person took the scissors and began the process of forgiveness, I saw each cord binding her to the corpse cut and it begin to fall away. Once each cord was loose, I saw God take the corpse from the person's back and place it onto Jesus' back. Forgiveness equals freedom from a burden that is not yours to carry. Romans 12:19 (The Message) states:

> 'Don't insist on getting even; that's not for you to do. "I'll do the judging", says God. "I'll take care of it."'

Dealing with consequences

Although forgiveness does not condone or excuse the wrong that has been done, it does not mean that a person's actions are without any consequences. Consequences are a healthy part of building relationships and navigating through life's challenges.

If someone consistently hurts you, puts you down, or abuses you, then yes, forgiveness is vital, but you need not keep putting yourself back into a relationship or situation that is damaging. Whilst you are in the process of forgiving a person, put in boundaries and practical strategies that ensure your contact with that person is minimal and that you have support if and when you need to interact with them.

A thief called nostalgia

Letting go off the past does not always just refer to negative experiences, pain or hurt. Sometimes, we need to make a decision not to fill our minds with nostalgia. Nostalgia is defined in the Collins' English dictionary as 'a yearning for the return of past circumstances'.

The emotion of nostalgia will take what are usually happy memories and make you feel as though nothing will ever match up to them. Nostalgia can distort your memories and leave you searching to replace or somehow relive those times again, to the detriment of enjoying the present or hoping for the future.

It's a different kind of reflection we can see in the rear-view mirror. It does not hurt because the past was so bad, but because the past was so good.

I had to teach my youngest son this recently when I found him in tears after watching a home video of a family holiday. I asked why he was crying and he told me that he had such a good time on that holiday, that every time he looked at the pictures, he wanted to make it happen again. He knew that was impossible and it made him sad.

I helped him identify this emotion called nostalgia and gently explained that it is not our friend. It comes dressed as a positive memory and then steals our hope for a better future. We cannot turn back time, our focus should be ahead not behind. However good or bad behind us looks, it is merely meant to be glanced at.

Having a rear-view mirror is useful, essential even. A quick glance in it lets us know it is safe to move forward but we must ensure that we don't allow it to distract us from the road ahead.

Another MMUK graduate, Amy, wrote these words:

> God's unconditional love, His Word and the wisdom of good people around me, taught me that my past is not my future, but also that my past isn't a complete write-off, as it demonstrates God's almighty power to overcome anything and everything. God has literally taken my past and recycled it to shape my future.

Summary: How to break free from the mirror of your past:

1. Recognise that you have been caught by it.

2. Accept that Jesus died so that you could be free from the past AND walk into a new future full of abundant life.

3. Ask His forgiveness for allowing the past to hold you captive.

4. Accept His forgiveness AND extend forgiveness to all those whose reflections you see when you look in that mirror of the past; those who hurt you, abused you, treated you badly and those who spoke negative things over you and about you.

5. Forgive yourself.

Prayer:

Father, I come before you now and ask that you would help me. Help me to be free from all that has happened to me; all the pain, the despair and the tormenting thoughts that go round and round.

Lord, I pray that you would make a way where there seems to be no way. I pray that you would take me by the hand and lead me out from the place that represents destruction and disaster.

Thank you for the cross. I ask that you forgive me for staying here in this place so long. I don't want to be trapped by this mirror any more. I forgive all those who have played a part in the pain I feel. I forgive ---------------------(list all the names of those you need to forgive). Lord, I choose to forgive myself too and release myself from false responsibility.

I choose to believe what your Word says about me. I choose to believe that you know the plans you have for me, plans to prosper me and not to harm me, plans to give me a hope and a future.

Thank you that as I work in partnership with your Holy Sprit, as I look within myself and turn remorse into resolve, I will walk away from the destruction that is behind and into the future you have planned and prepared for me.

In Jesus' name,

Amen

Chapter 3

Because You're Worth It:
The Full-Length Mirror

Most of us have a full-length mirror in the house somewhere. It's so we can see our whole outfit and check that we are fit for public display. This mirror helps us to answer questions such as: 'Does this top go with these trousers; does my bum look big in this skirt and should I wear the black shoes or the brown boots?'

The full-length mirror represents our self-esteem, our body image and sense of value. The reflection we see in this mirror makes us question whether we are presentable, acceptable and worthy.

When we look intently into this mirror, it can whisper untruths into our lives. It tells us that we are worthless, not up to standard and unacceptable. This mirror lies to us about our shape, our weight, our value and can undermine our self-esteem. We will only see what we think people think of us, what they have said to us, or what we imagine they are saying about us.

Our reflections will be based on the opinions of those around us and it'll change every day. We don't know who we are because our identity is caught up in other people's opinions of us and this mirror will trap us here if we let it.

The tell tale signs of this mirror's presence in our lives are clear: we build ourselves up when others like us or approve of us and we beat ourselves up when they don't.

When a compliment comes our way, it's like food; we can feed on it for days. The comment gets mulled over and over again and our self-esteem will be built on such positive comments.

But heaven forbid if someone should say something bad, or even worse, ignore us. Why didn't they say hello? What have I said? Have I upset them? What if they don't like me anymore? What if they tell their friends what they really think of me and then none of them likes me anymore? Is this top I'm wearing the right label, the right colour? Does this new hair colour make my face look fatter?

This mirror will influence everything you think about yourself, it will be your harshest critic and it is merciless. It will tell you that you fall short of people's expectations and it will leave you feeling under-valued, worthless and low; a failure.

At Mercy, we see the symptoms of hurt and broken lives every day; eating disorders, self harm, suicidal ideation and the anguish that comes from years of abuse.

But underneath all of those big branches of dysfunction lie roots that are giving life to those behaviours. It might surprise you to learn that the most common root cause of these problems is low self-esteem; an intense lack of value and worth.

Though not everyone who suffers from low self-esteem has tried to commit suicide and not everyone self harms or has depression, the symptoms of low self-esteem reach beyond the confines of the 'broken' girls we support through the Mercy Ministries programme - low self-esteem, low sense of worth and value is all around us in womanhood.

It's present in a woman's constant need to compare herself to others; it's present in our need to gossip about those around us and in our obsession with weight and diets to fit the accepted standard set by our society.

It's present in the woman who cannot stop eating because her sense of worth is so low that she seeks comfort in food because she doesn't love herself enough to be concerned about her health.

There are those women who spend themselves for others without a moment's pause, giving of self to the point where there is nothing left. There are those who will not spend a penny on themselves; not because they can't afford it but because they truly don't believe they are worth it. Dressing in old shapeless clothes to cover their shame.

These are all symptoms of deeper issues related to sense of worth and much of it comes from the lies told by the 'full length mirror'.

Is beauty only skin deep?

In 2005, Dove, one of Unilever's largest beauty brands, commissioned a report called 'The Real Truth About Beauty: A Global Report' to try to better understand the whole concept women have about beauty and its relationship with how we feel about ourselves.

It was carried out in 10 countries across the world and is the most extensive research ever carried out around this subject.

It found that only 2% of women would ever describe themselves as beautiful.

Surprised by this result the researchers looked into the definition of beauty that most women had responded to and found that they were defining the word 'beautiful' solely in terms of physical beauty.

The 21st century woman has totally bought into the concept that beauty is only physical appearance. This concept has come as a direct result of the power of mass media's portrayal of what is to be valued in a woman - the Barbie generation.

Yet did you know that if Barbie was a real person, she would likely be dead or dying from malnutrition? Her head circumference is the same as that of her waist, yet we give her to our daughters and reinforce the message that she is an image of perfection; an image of perfection that they will never be able to attain.

Beauty has become skin deep and even that has been airbrushed to perfection. 'Airbrushing' celebrities in magazines has become common practice and even the celebrities themselves cannot live up to the reproduction of their pictures. Actress Kate Winslet is reported to have asked the magazines to stop airbrushing her to extremes because she can't cope with the pressure it puts her under to look like that in real life.

Any deviation from the unrealistic and unachievable images we see in magazines, on our TV screens, on billboards or in the celebrity world is not considered 'beautiful' by most of us.

So when asked if they thought they were 'beautiful', it is no surprise that 98% of women said no.

This distorted mirror image of womanhood that the world is looking at, tells us that being 'physically attractive' (defined according to a strict criteria that few actually meet) equals feeling acceptable to society, which in turn equals happiness, fulfilment and contentment.

Conversely, not feeling beautiful (so 98% of us) equals unacceptable to society, which equals unhappiness, discontent and unfulfilment.

Being accepted by those around us is a basic need; we all want to find acceptance, but this will only happen in a healthy way when we have accepted ourselves first by looking into God's mirror and choosing to accept the image he presents to us, not by measuring ourselves according to what our society tells us we should look like.

We will never be able to control what people think or say about us, or to us. Many of us have been hurt by words spoken in anger, spitefulness or jealousy towards us.

But those words do not have the power to change who we are or how we behave unless we give them the power to do so. The moment we attach worth to what that person has said above what God has said about us, is the moment we give those words the power to destroy us.

Reinhard Bonnke, a prominent Christian speaker and evangelist said, 'If you value the praise of man, then the criticism of man will destroy you. Seek the honour of God, not the approval of man.'

It came as a huge shock to me when I discovered that I had been caught by this mirror after I had my first baby.

Before my pregnancy, I was confident in my body and the way I looked. I did not suspect how much of my confidence was built on that, instead of on knowing who I was in God and what he thought of me.

After my son was born I suddenly became worried about walking into a room full of (in my opinion) slim and attractive women. I hid my shape away in baggy clothes and mourned the loss of my prime.

I envied those who seemed to lose their 'baby weight' in minutes and went on faddy diets and crazy exercise routines to lose it. I had always been naturally slim and felt that everyone was watching my weight to see if I would return to my previous shape and size.

This was not helped by a comment made by an acquaintance shortly after I had my baby. 'What happened to you!?' he asked. 'You used to be so beautiful, now you look like... well, you know...'

He never finished the sentence, perhaps realising the mistake he had made, but the damage was done and my worst fears confirmed. I was no longer beautiful or attractive. My confidence plummeted.

We live in a society where physical looks have become what we measure our value upon and I was shocked to realise how much I had bought into the lie.

Under the knife

My lowest point came when I sat in the office of a cosmetic surgeon discussing an operation to turn back time on my breasts and get rid of some of the extra skin my 10lb baby had left me with.

I sat there while he told me the risks, which included anything from mild infection to a seriously adverse reaction that could permanently disfigure me. Was I still happy to sign the disclaimer and pay the deposit on the small fortune it would cost?

I walked out of that room, feeling so confused, low and miserable. I asked God if having the surgery was ok. All he said to me was, "Does it really matter that much?" My initial response was, "Yes, it does actually", but I knew that God's question to me was an invitation to discover what it means to truly know that beauty is so much more than what your body looks like.

I am not against cosmetic surgery, but I believe that our motives for having it done really need to be examined. I have friends who have had it done. It was the right decision for them and I supported them in it but it would have been the wrong choice for me.

God used this experience to reveal to me what the foundations of my self-esteem, confidence and sense of self-worth were built upon.

Many of us have based our sense of identity on what people have said or done to us or on the issues we have to deal with in life: disappointment, abuse, divorce, debt, bullies, loss.

It might not be your physical beauty that bothers you. Maybe for you it is people-pleasing and you only feel good about yourself when people like you. Or maybe it's compromising what you know is right because it doesn't fit in with the status quo. Perhaps your life is being ruled by the needs of others.

Or maybe you hate yourself because the people who should have loved you didn't and your self-image was shaped by rough hands.

The fact is even if every person who is supposed to love you does and even if you've never experienced abuse or hurt, your security and sense of value is still at risk if it's rooted in the wrong things.

Even though I had a loving husband, a beautiful baby and great friends, their love did not protect me from an attack on my self-esteem. Few are immune to this mirror of lies until they choose to shift their gaze and start to look at their true reflection in the mirror of God's word.

The distorted reflection of the full-length mirror, will entice us to set our value by our own feelings or opinions of ourselves in comparison to others. Our worth is then determined by lies we have chosen to believe. The very foundations that our lives are built on become unstable when we give power to lies instead of embracing the truth of what God has said.

We build our lives on the sands of low self-esteem and worthlessness and the Bible tells us when our lives are built on sand, the storms of life will come and wipe us out.

Jesus told us to build our house on the Rock. Our lives, all that flows out of us needs to have a firm foundation.

That firm foundation is made up of a sense of identity in Christ, and a sense of worth and value based on the word of truth - and nothing else.

He will begin to change us from the inside out; he will start to make sure that we are building on the Rock by speaking to us about our true value and worth.

God's mirror will show you your true value

God's mirror works in direct contrast to the false reflection of the 'full length' mirror. His mirror will teach us that our sense of significance and value comes from understanding that we can never increase or decrease in value to God. It is set - not by who we are or what we do, but by who God is and what Christ did for us.

Value is established by how much someone is willing to pay and Jesus paid with his life. Our worth and value is non-negotiable, we can't enter into discussion with God about worth, it is set not by who we are or what we have done but by who he is and what he has done for us.

God's mirror, his word, will tell us exactly what we are worth and how loved we are. Its reflection is clear, unchanging and not dependent on whether we think we deserve it or not.

God's word is very clear about our beauty, our value and our worth. Just to prove my point, let me 'scripture blast' you.

Jeremiah 1:5
Before I formed you in the womb, I knew you, before you were born I set you apart.

Exodus 19:5 (Amplified Bible)

[5]Now therefore, if you will listen to My voice in truth and keep My covenant, then you shall be My own special treasure from among and above all peoples; for all the earth is Mine.

Psalm 139 (The Message)

Oh yes, you shaped me first inside, then out;
you formed me in my mother's womb.
I thank you, High God—you're breathtaking!
Body and soul, I am marvelously made!
I worship in adoration—what a creation!
You know me inside and out,
you know every bone in my body;
You know exactly how I was made, bit by bit,
how I was sculpted from nothing into something.

Like an open book, you watched me grow from conception to birth;all the stages of my life were spread out before you,
The days of my life all prepared before I'd even lived one day.

Ephesians 1:11

In him we were also chosen, having been predestined according to the plan of him who works out everything in conformity with the purpose of his will.

Deuteronomy 7:7-8 (NLT):

The Lord did not choose you and lavish His love on you because you were larger or greater than any other nations, for you were the smallest of all nations. It was simply because the Lord loves you.

Romans 9:25 (The Message):

I'll call nobodies and make them somebodies. I'll call the unloved and make them beloved.

Ephesians 1:3-5

Long before he laid down earth's foundations, he had us in mind, had settled on us as the focus of his love, to be made whole and holy by his love. Long, long ago he decided to adopt us into his family through Jesus Christ (what pleasure he took in planning this!).

I think these scriptures clearly show we are the focus of his love, he personally created and knit us together and he thinks we are beautiful.

Long before we ever lived, he planned to adopt us into his family through Jesus' death and resurrection. He decided to pay the ultimate price so that we could be his. He saw us. He saw our faces and thought we were worth it. Our value is set.

Our sense of value can been eroded: by ourselves, by others' words, actions and neglect or by the guilt we feel from the things we have done. But God has determined that our own perception of our worth doesn't change our value to him.

There's an old illustration that demonstrates this concept beautifully.

Imagine that I offered you a £50 note. You would want to accept it because it's valuable,. It's worth £50 exactly, no more or no less.

Before I handed it over I told you that this £50 had a past. It had been used to pay for sex with a prostitute. It was stolen from a man who was beaten and his blood was still on it. It had been rolled up and had drugs sniffed through it and had spent many years hidden under a mattress forgotten by the one who owned it. It's torn, stained and still has all the residue of filth stuck on it from the awful ways it had been used in the past.

Would you still want it? Of course you would, but why? The fact is: it's still worth £50 no matter what is has been used for because its value is set by its maker. Its value is not determined by what has happened to it, what it looks like or how it feels.

God didn't use our imperfections to negotiate a lower price. He paid in full, one Son, one price, one value. He paid the same for you as he did for the most holy and perfect person you can think of. Our worth to God is non-negotiable.

Someone once said that God doesn't love us because we are valuable; we are valuable because he loves us.

Joy, one of the graduates of the Mercy Ministries' programme, was someone who was trapped by false mirrors, especially the full-length mirror. Her life was so shaped by people's comments, her low self-worth and her need to people-please that she resorted to drastic measures. This is Joy's story:

"I was brought up in a Christian home having parents who faithfully took me to church every week, so I always had a basic understanding of God.

However, from the age of about 7 for nearly 10 years, I was sexually, physically and verbally abused by a teacher and other male figures in my life.

I first self-harmed when I was about eleven years old, but a few years later it became a part of my everyday routine. I would burn or cut myself in order to damage the vile person I thought I was. All I saw in me was marred by the past that I was letting define me. I never believed I could love myself.

I viewed myself through people's opinions of me and so, after being called fat, I began attempting to make myself sick as well as engaging in periods of self-starvation. My mind was overwhelmed with darkness and life seemed unendingly bleak.

On September 12th, 2007, with the awesome support that I received from those around me at home, I entered Mercy Ministries UK; broken, hurting, miserable and desperate for a way out of the darkness that had become my existence. Stepping through those doors was God lifting me out of the slimy pit and setting my feet on a rock and giving me a firm place to stand.

At Mercy, God began to renew my mind to who I am in Christ and I can truly say that I love what I see when I look at myself now. There's beauty inside and out that I can finally see with my own eyes. I'm confident, full of joy and I have a deep-rooted hope that will never cease.

My past can no longer steal my future. My life is an absolute reflection of the truth having set me free. Instead of planning my suicide, I now cherish every breath I take and I'm going to embrace every moment God gives me."

Joy's outlook on life is an example of what transformation can take place once you move your gaze from the full-length mirror and stop building your life on the shifting sand of people-pleasing and low self- esteem.

In my own life, I know that my confidence, self-esteem and sense of value no longer comes from how people perceive me or whether I am happy with the shape of my body, my clothes or my hair. My confidence is firmly rooted in who my Father says I am and what he thinks about me and I now know the safest place to build my self-esteem is on the Rock.

There is a song by a band called 'Barlow Girl' which has become an anthem for many of our girls on the Mercy Ministries programme because it talks about this journey of learning to see our reflection through God's eyes.

Mirror, Mirror on the wall,
Have I got it?
'Cause Mirror you've always told me who I am.
I'm finding it's not easy, to be perfect,
So sorry you won't define me,
Sorry you don't own me.

Who are you to tell me
That I'm less than what I should be?
Who are you? Who are you?

I don't need to listen to the list of things I should be.
I won't try, I won't try.

Mirror, I am seeing a new reflection,
I'm looking into the eyes of he who made me
And to him I have beauty beyond compare,
I know he defines me.

Copyright Barlow/Barlow/Barlow © Word Music 2003

Let's keep our eyes on the one who made us and let's let him be the one who defines us, not the false mirror that demands the perfection we can never attain.

Summary: How to break free from the mirror of low self-esteem and people-pleasing:

1. Ask God's forgiveness for building your self-esteem, sense of value and acceptance on other things, rather than on his word.

2. Choose to renew your mind. Find out in the Word what God's truth says. As an example, in Appendix I are listed some common 'false reflections' with God's truth written underneath. This is a very practical, hands-on and deliberate way to renew your mind and you can use some of those statements as starting points for writing ones that are relevant to you.

Prayer:

Father, I thank you for creating me and giving me life. Thank you that you loved me enough to send your Son to die for me.

Lord, forgive me for not being in agreement with your word about my worth and value. Forgive me for being more concerned with what people think than what you think.

From today, I choose to start renewing my mind and bringing it into alignment with what your thoughts are regarding me.

Help me Holy Spirit to clearly see the lies I have believed about myself. Help me to see the truth about my identity and worth as I look into the mirror of your word.

In Jesus' name,
Amen.

Chapter 4

Who's The Fairest of Them All?
The Dance Studio Mirror

It was like watching a scene from the 80's TV show 'Fame'. A group of sweaty dancers rehearsed the same steps again and again, to the sound of a piano and the voice of a teacher shouting correction and encouragement in equal measures. My friend Fi was in the rehearsal bending, turning, jumping and getting ready for that evening's performance. She has been a ballerina for years and is used to facing the rigorous demands of the dance studio mirror.

At the end of the rehearsal I ask her what it's like to have to look at herself in the mirror all day. She thinks for a moment and then makes a profound statement, 'Actually, it's not looking at myself in the mirror that is difficult, it's looking at myself compared to the other dancers that is the hardest part.'

And so I present to you the 'Dance Studio Mirror'. This mirror is all about our status and position in comparison to those around us. This mirror will only show us a false reflection of our identity, one defined by our performance compared to others

It's an unfortunate female trait to compare ourselves to those around us and usually we mark ourselves down. We feel depressed because everyone else has managed to lose their pregnancy weight, keep their house spotless, organise their children's birthday party, get a job, go to college and the list goes on.

We look in the dance studio mirror and watch everyone else's work-out. We see how competent they look compared to us. They seem to be far more graceful in how they handle life; they look more together than us, more attractive than us. As we allow comparison to invade our life we feel under pressure because everyone else's show seems much more impressive than ours.

What we seldom realise is that those we compare ourselves to are also looking at us and feeling inadequate in the same way.

The wicked stepmother in the story 'Snow White' was driven to destruction by one thing - looking in the wrong mirror. Looking into the mirror of comparison led to insecurity and jealousy, and eventually her jealousy led her to destruction. In the same way, many people look into the dance studio mirror and ask, 'Mirror, mirror on the wall, who is the fairest, richest, most successful, best dressed, most spiritual, most generous and kindest of them all? Is it me, or is it her?

The dance studio mirror will always show you an image of yourself that doesn't match up to those around. It will erode your sense of self-worth and confidence by making you feel you don't measure up as you constantly compare yourself to others.

Before I had children, I was a school teacher, earning a good salary and having the enviable status of 'professional'. Once I had my first baby however, I realised that staying at home with my child had seriously affected the value others placed on my contribution to society.

I remember during this time applying for car insurance online and as I filled out the required information, I came to the box that asked for my occupation. As I was no longer teaching I scrolled down the list of options, of professions that my car insurance company validated as legitimate, until I came to a sudden halt at 'housewife - no occupation'.

As I grudgingly selected this option, I came to the sad realisation that my status had dropped in our society's viewpoint to 'just a housewife' and I found that it caused within me a pressure to conform, to 'be someone' and 'do something' and it began to erode my sense of identity. I was looking in the wrong mirror.

This dance studio mirror will tell us that we need to perform; to match up to the standards people have set for us; we must become all that 'they' expect us to become. However, we should never find our worth in a status, job title or in how society views us. We need to realise that when God looks at us, he sees only us. He made each of us unique, therefore nothing and no-one compares to you!

God's mirror reflection shows only you

There are some verses in Galatians, which I love because they describe God's true reflection of us. It says in Galatians 6[8],

> 'Make a careful exploration of who you are and the work you
> have been given, and then sink yourself into that. Don't be
> impressed with yourself. Don't compare yourself with others.
> Each of you must take responsibility for doing the creative best
> you can with your own life.'

This is such a freedom bringing scripture. It says 'you have to do the creative best with your own life.' That means you have to *do* your best, not *be* the best!

You don't have to be better than anyone else - you can just be you. Nothing you do for God will be compared to what

---

[8] Galatians 6:3-5 The Message

others have done for him, he just sees you in relation to you. How liberating it is to realise you are in a one-woman race!

This truth releases us to help others, because when there is no need to compare, we are no longer threatened by or jealous of them. When we stop being in competition we release one another to be the person God is shaping us to be. When we have a clear understanding of our own test, our own tasks, and our own callings, it gives a confidence that comes from knowing who we are in Christ: a Godly confidence that isn't dependent on the opinions of others.

Comparison creates insecurity; it feeds a lack of confidence in ourselves and makes us question our own identity and relationship with God.

Joy, one of the Mercy graduates I quoted earlier, said this about it;

> 'I was humiliated by teachers who seemed to find delight in mocking me in front of my peers. I never felt good enough and often compared myself to others. I lost all sense of who I was, as my identity revolved around my pain and the lies that had been part of my life for so long.'

And another graduate, Cath, said this;

> 'Before I came to Mercy, I had such low self-esteem; over 15 years' worth of thoughts of not being worth anything, not being as good as everyone else (comparison) and not reaching the mark. I had such control issues, but daily I had to make a choice to trust and surrender my life to God. As I worked through forgiving others who'd hurt me, I was released!

A massive lesson I learnt during my time at Mercy Ministries was not to always believe my very dippy emotions and feelings - and to reach higher and believe what God says about me over the circumstance I'm in - as well as not comparing myself to others all the time."

The story of the prodigal son is an illustration of how much harm the power of comparison can do. A family has been reunited after thinking they had lost their youngest child. His parents were rejoicing at his return, but the older brother refused to join the welcoming committee.

This brother was the one who had stayed at home. He had worked hard for his family and had not let his father down. He hadn't run off to squander his inheritance like his younger sibling. He just faithfully got on with what he was meant to be doing.

All was well until the younger brother returned. Now there was another person in the dance hall mirror and the older brother began to compare.

Suddenly the older brother became consumed with jealousy, grumbling, moaning and complaining about the way he had been treated until his father spoke up in Luke 15[9];

> 'My son,' the father said, 'you are always with me, and everything I have is yours. But we had to celebrate and be glad, because this brother of yours was dead and is alive again; he was lost and is found.'

---

[9] Luke 15:31-32 NIV

In other words, 'Stop looking at what your brother has and understand that you have everything you need right at your fingertips!'

You see, once the party was over, the younger son would have to start all over again to earn back the inheritance he had spent. This was an important fact that the older brother had obviously overlooked.

The older brother's faithfulness meant that his inheritance was intact and he had access to all of his father's wealth. Yet all he could see in the dance hall studio mirror was that his brother had got away with so much compared to him, and his attitude became selfish, ungrateful and petty.

Comparison will rob us of our relationship with God if we become bitter about what we do or do not have compared to others. Comparison will rob us of our future when we disqualify ourselves because of what we feel we lack compared to others. Comparison will rob us of our peace when we allow others' lives to influence our view of our own. Its distorted reflection will make you think you are empty-handed when in fact you have full access to the Father, his blessing and your inheritance, right at your fingertips.

Protected by gratitude

Gratitude is an antidote to comparison. One of the most effective ways to combat the thief of comparison, is to cloak ourselves in gratitude.

When we choose gratitude over comparison we agree with the truth that everything good in our lives has come from God. His word says that he gives us every good and perfect gift. Sometimes the difference between receiving or not receiving the gift is our attitude of thankfulness.

Luke 17 tells the story of ten lepers who asked Jesus to heal them. Only one of them returned to give thanks for the healing they had received and Jesus told him, 'Arise, go on your way, your faith has made you whole[10].

All of them received a good and perfect gift of healing, but nine of them only ever knew what it was like to be healed from leprosy. The one who had a thankful heart experienced the joy of being made whole.

When you look at what God did for that one leper compared to the other nine it may seem unfair. However, the same offer was open to all, but the outcome was determined by their attitudes, thoughts and responses to God. It is the same in our own lives.

A mirror can only ever reflect what we put in front of it, so the easy answer to avoiding the dance studio mirror is not to look in it. By refusing to enter into comparison and choosing to be thankful even in times of adversity and lack, we instantly shatter its power. Our confidence is secure when it is built on the identity we see in God's word, not on the one we have perceived in comparison to our peers.

Isaiah 1:16 says this, 'Stop doing wrong, learn to do right.' In the case of this particular mirror, I believe this is exactly what is needed. Stop looking in the mirror of comparison and learn to cloak yourself in thankfulness. I promise you this reflection will no longer have any power over you, in Jesus' Name.

Summary: How to break free from the Dance Studio Mirror:

1. Repent for viewing yourself in comparison to others.

2. Every time you feel down, jealous or discontent because of what others have or are achieving in life;

---

[10] Luke 17:19

or when your emotions tell you that you are a failure because others seem to always succeed, recognise the lie.   Then choose to remain thankful in all circumstances. (1 Thessalonians 5:18)

3. If it helps, write a list of the things you are thankful for and remind yourself of this when the mirror reflection presents itself. The false reflection will shatter.

Prayer:

Lord, thank you for saving me. Thank you for taking disease, affliction, misery, pain, poverty, brokenness and every sin that this world is bound by on your own shoulders.

Thank you that I now have access to all your kingdom has to offer. Thank you that when you look at me, you see only me and not my friends, my family or anyone else, just me. Lord, help me to do the same - to see myself in relation to you, not in comparison with others.

Father, I ask that you forgive my attitude of comparison and the jealousy and insecurity that has plagued me; and I ask that you would make my spirit sensitive to recognising when I slip back into these attitudes.

I commit to entering your gates with thanksgiving and choose to shatter the mirror of comparison by remaining thankful at all times. Help me to do this by your Spirit.

In Jesus' Name,
Amen

Chapter 5

Tales of the Unexpected:
The Shop Window Mirror

It is the day of your all-important, dream job interview. You've spent ages choosing just the right outfit, hairstyle and make-up and you look great. You are feeling confident, the sun is shining and the train is running on time.

All of a sudden, it starts to rain and you realise you left your umbrella at home. The wind is blowing a gale and you realise you also forgot to use waterproof mascara. With a sense of rising panic, you realise that although the train isn't late, you are. You break into a run and trip up on the uneven pavement. With a sinking feeling you look down and see a broken heel dangling from your shoe and a large rip in your tights.

As you hobble past a shop window, you catch a glimpse of your reflection and it confirms all of your worst fears. Your 'up-do' is down, your mascara is giving you a 'gothic chick' look instead of the 'capable professional' look you were aiming for. With one heel on and one heel off, your confident 'I-have-it-all-together' look is as washed out as your hopes.

All that time and energy spent on getting ready, all your optimism and hopes are dashed as this unexpected course of events. The shop window reflection confirms it, catches you off-guard and steals your opportunity. You turn around, watch the train leave without you and decide that the job clearly wasn't meant to be yours, so you might as well give up.

It's the mirror of our circumstances, the unpredictability of life, and if we're looking in this one, then our sense of identity, value, strength and purpose will be determined by whether our life is going well or not.

It sounds like this:

> 'If my life is good, then God is good and so I feel good about myself. I'm a daughter of the King and he loves me. But if life is bad, then I'm a terrible person. This must be punishment and God doesn't love me anymore. He has forgotten me and maybe I'm not even saved!'

The thoughts, feelings and emotions that capture our attention when life throws us a curve-ball are what determine whether the outcome of those circumstances will kill us or make us stronger.

The world we live in has rough terrain called hurt, pain, fear, abuse, betrayal, disappointment, rebellion, mistrust and injustice.

Yet, there is a popular misconception amongst many that says as Christians, we are entitled to a problem-free life. Hardship, challenges, trouble and disappointment are all part of the 'world of the wicked' and as such, if we are 'good', we are immune from these things.

Consequently, they spend much time and effort being good, sticking to all the rules, which is why when trouble comes, they think that they have somehow let God down and that this is their punishment. Alternatively, they begin to believe that God is in the habit of sending pain and hurt to teach his people how to behave.

This is not true because God is not the author of our pain. Jesus died and rose again so that we would not need to jump through hoops to gain God's favour. His grace covers us, and as a result, we are able to stand before him completely righteous without need to prove ourselves. God does not throw you into the fire to teach you that it's hot. That's not the kind of Father he is.

When Jesus commissioned us to go out into all of the world and preach the good news, He knew the world would not give us a nice smooth, tarmac road but mud, rocks, hills and valleys.

When we face trouble in our lives it can be caused by a number of things. We can be the victims of other people's bad choices or we can be experiencing the consequences of our own poor decisions. Trouble comes from hurt people hurting people and from living in a world that does not know God. Trouble comes from an enemy who kills, steals and destroys in every way he can.

When bad things happen to good people

In 2 Corinthians 11:23-28 (The Message). Paul the apostle writes[11]:

> *I've worked much harder, been jailed more often, beaten up more times than I can count, and at death's door time after time. I've been flogged five times with the Jews' thirty-nine lashes, beaten by Roman rods three times, pummelled with rocks once. I've been shipwrecked three times, and immersed in the open sea for a night and a day. In hard journeys travelling year in and year out, I've had to ford rivers, fend off robbers, struggle with friends, struggle with foes. I've been at risk in the city, at risk in the country, endangered by desert sun and sea storm, and betrayed by those I thought were my brothers. I've known drudgery and hard labour, many a long and lonely night without sleep, many a missed meal, blasted by the cold,*

---

[11] 2 Corinthians 11:23-28 The Message

> *naked to the weather. And that's not the half of it.'*

Paul laid his life down for the faith; he was a good person, a godly person and yet bad things happened to him and around him. Just like our lives can be, the landscape of his life was full of the hills and valleys of adversity and challenge.

The good news is that God never intended us to face the hills and valleys of our lives alone. He never intended for us to face a storm without a way to silence it. Paul understood this and went on to write about God's response to his troubles in 2 Corinthians:

> *'My grace is enough; it's all you need. My strength comes into its own in your weakness.'*

Paul goes on to write:

> *'Once I heard that, I was glad to let it happen. I quit focusing on the handicap and began appreciating the gift. It was a case of Christ's strength moving in on my weakness. Now I take limitations in stride, and with good cheer, these limitations that cut me down to size—abuse, accidents, opposition, bad breaks. I just let Christ take over! And so the weaker I get, the stronger I become.'* [12]

We need to understand that we do not have what it takes to navigate rough terrain in our own strength. But we can do it when we let Christ take over.

I faced one of these testing times in 2008 as I listened in shock to my Doctor tell me that the lump they had just done a biopsy on would be sent away for tests. I had to wait a

---

[12] 2 Corinthians 12: 7-10

week for the results and there was about a 50 percent chance that I had cancer.

During this unexpected situation, I had one of those God dreams that you never forget. In my dream I was reading Psalm 23:5, 'You prepare a table before me in the presence of my enemies'.

I saw myself dining at a huge round table with Wisdom on my right and Strength on my left. Around the table were seated Love, Hope, Faith, Joy and Peace. They were all interacting with me and chatting, as part of my circle of companions.

Then I became aware that over in the corner of the room were three shadowy figures called Fear, Worry and Unbelief and I asked God why they were there.

God replied saying, 'Life on earth is a public place much like a restaurant, this is why the table is prepared in the presence of your enemies; Fear, Unbelief and Worry will always linger on the fringes of life, BUT who sits at YOUR table is by invitation only. Be very careful who you choose to keep company with.'

I could see that each time I looked over to where the three figures were huddled, they would look up to see if I was inviting them over. They inched closer and closer, peeking in over the goings on at my table, trying to see if I was giving them permission to take a seat.

Then, as I looked around the table, I saw that there were only enough seats for the companions I already had. God said, 'Your friends cannot stay if you give their seat to one of the three.' At that moment I saw Fear standing behind Faith, looking to see if I would give the nod and ask Faith to give up her seat for him.

This dream showed me that the battle I faced would be won or lost in my mind. Faith is a powerful weapon, and the first thing the enemy will try to do is separate you from the companions God has given to you to do your thought life with.

During the wait for my test results I learnt what it means to take every thought captive and make it obedient to Christ. A process was taking place inside of me as I chose not to let the unexpected reflection of the 'shop window' stop me in my tracks and throw me off course.

I didn't have cancer, thank God, but I still won a battle. I won the battle for my peace of mind as I triumphed over Fear, and Faith stayed at my table.

Defeating fear

Our deepest convictions about God are revealed during times of trial and adversity when life can feel very uncertain. Corrie ten Boom once said, "Never be afraid to trust an unknown future to a known God."

Yet so many of us fear the future. We fear what may or may not happen. When life is going well, we worry that the bubble will burst and when life is bad, we blame ourselves, God, those around us, or the church. By doing this we hand the enemy our peace.

I really struggled with this kind of fear after my first child was born. I loved him so much that I was frightened that something bad might happen to him and became obsessed with his safety.

Maybe some of you mothers would be able to identify with this - nights of sleeplessness were caused not just by his needing feeding but also by my fear. Was he breathing, was he too hot, too cold, should he lie on his back, his front, his side?

You see, not long before my child was born, a couple close to us had lost their son to a still-birth at 29 weeks. They were the perfect Christian couple, leaders in the church and kind, good-hearted servants of God. Yet they lost their baby. As far as I could see, there was no safety, no assurance for me. If it could happen to them I thought it could happen to me, and suddenly I was caught by that shop window reflection.

God's answer to questions about our future health, wealth and security will always be the same. If you ask him, like I did, he will probably just hold his hand out to you, smile affectionately and whisper, 'Do you trust me?'

When we don't trust him, we feed Fear. When we question God's character and his intentions towards us, we allow Unbelief and Worry to dine with us.

There was a story I read amidst my battle with fear for my son's well-being, which helped me understand what God was after.

It was about a couple whose baby daughter had been rushed to hospital with meningitis. They prayed and prayed and thankfully, in the morning, she had made it through the night and was going to recover. As the man and his wife were praising and thanking God for healing their precious baby and protecting her, they felt God say, 'Would you still praise me if she had died?'

If we really know God, know that he is good all the time, know that all things work together for the good of those who love him and are called according to his purpose, then we do not have to fear an unknown future. It will not necessarily be without pain or heartache, but should difficult circumstances come we will not have to face them alone.

The Bible also says that we are more than conquerors[13]. Do you know the difference between a conqueror and being more than a conqueror? A conqueror wins a battle, but someone who is more than a conqueror wins the war.

---

[13] Romans 8:37 NIV

We are fighting a war for our peace, our trust in God, our intimacy and our relationship with him. Life's circumstances can conspire against us to keep us far from him, distrusting his intentions and fearing the future. We must choose to start speaking out the truth of God's word, and choose to get to know him more, even through life's challenges.

Choosing joy in the trial

I clearly recollect a time when this unexpected shop window reflection' caught me head-on. An unexpected situation occurred which had the potential to devastate everything I had worked so hard for. That day as I caught my reflection in the shop window of my life, I could see my hopes and dreams fading fast.

I recall standing in my kitchen buttering bread. As I stood there, waves of despair crashed over me with such ferocity that I literally felt like I was drowning emotionally.

During this emotional onslaught I heard the whisper of the Holy Spirit, quiet but intense. He said, 'Right now, at this very moment - choose joy.'

It was probably one of the most ridiculous things God had ever said to me. Joy was the furthest thing from my mind and the emotions I was experiencing were so opposed to joy, I had no idea how to choose it.

But as I stood there, an old Sunday school song came to mind. It goes something like this;

> Rejoice in the Lord always, again I say rejoice.
> Rejoice in the Lord always, again I say rejoice.
> Rejoice, rejoice, again I say rejoice.
> Rejoice, rejoice, again I say rejoice.

I started to hum it softly, then to whisper it until within a few minutes I was pacing up and down my kitchen, waving a breadknife in my hand singing the command over myself. My husband walked in on me at that moment and swiftly did a U-turn - he knows when to leave me alone!

As I sang and refused to let the negative emotions drown out my voice, I could feel joy begin to bubble up inside and with it came strength. This was not a joy that I had generated because I had no reason to be joyful. The joy that bubbled up came straight from God. All I did was choose to make room for it. As it says in Nehemiah 8[14]: 'The joy of the Lord is your strength.'

Within minutes of this happening another scripture came to mind. It says in James 1[15]:

> 'Dear brothers and sisters, when troubles come your way, consider it an opportunity for great joy. For you know that when your faith is tested, your endurance has a chance to grow. So let it grow, for when your endurance is fully developed, you will be perfect and complete, needing nothing.'

God's mirror will make you laugh at the days to come

Proverbs 31 shows us a mirror image of a woman of God, it says in v 25-26: 'She is clothed with strength and dignity, she can laugh at the days to come.'

So, the Proverbs 31 woman is laughing at the days to come, even though she has no idea whether those days contain good circumstances or bad circumstances. She knows that bad news may come but she has no fear of it.

When we choose to look in God's mirror, our laughter is not dependant on our circumstances.

---

[14] Nehemiah 8:10 NIV
[15] James 1:2-4 NIV

Our laughter will come from the knowledge of God in our lives, from the sense of security and comfort that he brings. He is your rock, your deliverer, your tower of strength and when you look in his mirror, you may not be able to see all of your future but you can be confident that whether there be good times or bad times ahead, God is God and he is good.

When you learn that, you know that you will be able to laugh at the days to come, because when you look in his mirror, you will see not just who you are but who he is and if you choose to believe it, no circumstance will ever take you away from your sense of identity and security.

Paul the apostle knew this, as it says in Philippians 4:11-13:

> *'I have learned to be content whatever the circumstances. I know what it is to be in need, and I know what it is to have plenty. I have learned the secret of being content in any and every situation, whether well fed or hungry, whether living in plenty or in want. I can do everything through him who gives me strength.'*

Philippians 4[16] also tells us that if we learn to rejoice in the Lord always, whether the circumstances we face are good or bad, we are promised a certain type of peace. It says:

> *'And God's peace shall be yours, that tranquil state of a soul assured of its salvation through Christ, and so fearing nothing from God and being content with its earthly lot of whatever sort that is, that peace] which transcends all understanding shall garrison and mount guard over your hearts and minds in Christ Jesus.'*

---

[16] Philippians 4

God's peace is the only kind of peace that will get you through life in an unpredictable world that does not guarantee you a pain-free journey.

In other words, God's peace surpasses the reflection of the 'Shop Window' that would have you believe you are a lost cause. His peace is not dependent on what your reflection looks like or what your circumstances are. His peace protects you as you look at those circumstances and decide to praise him anyway.

I believe the early church found that kind of peace when they sang his praises as they were being fed to the lions. I believe Esther found that peace when she said, 'If I perish, I perish.' I believe James found that peace when he told us to, 'Count it pure joy when you face trials of many kinds.' I believe Mary found that kind of peace when she said, 'Be it unto me as you have said.'

I believe that when she had lost everything, Ruth had that peace when she said to Naomi, 'Wherever you go I go, your people will be my people and your God, my God.' And I believe Jesus had that peace when he said 'not my will but yours be done'.

We can have that peace when we refuse to let our lives be shaken by circumstances and instead say, 'I trust you Lord, you are good to me, I know I am not alone in this trial and I choose to rejoice.'

When the unexpected happens, when crisis hits your life, that's when the mirror of his word will show you not just your reflection, but his too. As you gaze at him, as you draw close to him, it will be his peace that guards your heart and your mind.

Debbie, a Mercy Ministries graduate, learnt what it means to deal with the 'Shop Window Reflection'. This is her story:

'Born and raised in a Christian home, I was taught that

God was my protector, my provider, my Father. I grew up listening to and learning about God. I knew the Bible stories and I believed that God was everything the Bible said about Him.

But when I was 12 years old, it seemed that all I had been taught was a lie. I was manipulated into a full sexual relationship with a drug dealer 10 years my senior. He introduced me to the 'benefits' of getting high on cannabis and gradually he groomed and seduced me into a sexually abusive relationship with him.

Suddenly, the normal Christian life I had been brought up in, changed dramatically. Every day for three years was the same, hidden with the same lie that all was fine, but it wasn't. I got into fights, began cutting myself and even tried to commit suicide, but it didn't work. I felt like I couldn't tell anyone because I thought it was all my fault.

I was caught in a spiral of helplessness and shame, and my anger burned against a God who should have protected me, who could have stopped it or told someone about the abuse I was suffering. I renounced God and vowed to live my life outside of Him.

I had no hope, no future, no peace, no truth; just pain, despair, shame and the lies of the enemy tormenting my mind constantly. The root causes of my pain were not being dealt with and I desperately needed help.

I remembered a book my sister gave me about Mercy Ministries, and as I read it, I knew there was hope; I knew there was a place that could help me. A few months later, I was on a plane to Nashville, Tennessee, hoping that this place I had read so much about could help me to interpret the pain inside and get to the root cause of my anger, drug abuse, rebellion and self-harm.

At Mercy, I learnt that we all have personal choices, and that sadly some of us become the victims of other people's bad choices. God did not send the abuse because the Bible teaches that every good and perfect gift comes from God and abuse is neither of those things. The enemy comes to steal, kill and destroy, and so abuse in all its forms has its roots well and truly in his territory.

I now know that God has provided freedom from the abuse through the power of the cross and redemption. I have learnt to forgive, and in doing so, have found that the hurt, pain and destruction I was facing have been processed and dealt with, with God at my side.

Now, 8 years after I graduated Mercy Ministries of America, I am happily married, serving in my local church, expecting my first child after nearly three years of trying to conceive and I have the privilege of working as the Programme Director of Mercy Ministries UK. Only God can bring about that kind of transformation!'

Summary: How to break free from the Shop Window Reflection:

1. Determine in advance that your identity and value will only be found in what God's word says about you, so that you will not be deceived by the mirror of circumstances.

2. Be careful about who you invite to sit at the table of your thought life. Faith and Fear cannot sit in the

same place. When you feed faith by believing God's word, you starve fear.

3.   Take every thought captive on a daily basis so that an unexpected reflection in the 'shop window' will not be able to throw you off course. Write out key verses that apply to your life and situation and start declaring these truths over the circumstances you're facing. Make a choice to believe God's voice over the voice of adversity.

Prayer:

Lord, thank you that your love surpasses human love. That your love is not dependent upon whether or not I feel worthy of it; that it is constant, without beginning or end no matter what circumstances I face.

Thank you for the promise that you WILL make ALL things work for good for those who love you. Help me to see you at work in every situation, in the calm and in the storms.

Help me to not hide away from the adversities that come my way but to walk through them holding your hand, secure in the knowledge that your strength is made perfect in my weakness, that you are growing me through situations that the enemy meant for harm and are leading me to a higher level of faith, trust and joy.

Father, show me the patterns of thought in my mind that are not of you. I want to get rid of everything that hinders me from grabbing hold of my present and my future. Show me what you say about me. I choose today to feed faith and starve fear.

I choose to look adversity in the face and I choose to declare joy over my circumstances. I laugh at the days to come and declare you are greater than my troubles, because the bigger I see you, the smaller they become. Thank you for your truth that sets me free.

In Jesus' name,

Amen.

Chapter 6

The Compact Mirror
Know, Believe, Do

There is one type of mirror which every girl should carry. It can be taken with you wherever you go and can be used whenever you need it.

It's there in emergencies, as well as for the odd touch up and is one of the essentials to be found in every woman's handbag. It's a compact mirror and this is the kind of mirror God's word is to our lives; always there inside our hearts in case of emergencies, or simply because we want to check something - easy to get to, often used. Just like you can't see your reflection in a mirror unless you look in it, you can't see your true reflection unless you look in the true mirror that is his word.

Let's remind ourselves of what it says about God's compact mirror in James 1[17]

> *Do not merely listen to the word, and so deceive yourselves. Do what it says. Anyone who listens to the word but does not do what it says is like a man who looks at his face in a mirror and, after looking at himself, goes away and immediately forgets what he looks like. But the man who looks intently into the perfect law that gives freedom, and continues to do this, not forgetting what he has heard, but doing it - he will be blessed in what he does.'*

---

[17] James 1:22-25 NIV

It couldn't be clearer; if we want to know what we really look like there is only one mirror that can reflect our true image that is not distorted by our past or our insecurities. There is only one mirror that does not compare us with others or change what it shows us, depending on our circumstances. It is the mirror of God's word. Its reflection is constant, it's unchanging and it shows us who we really are.

Know, believe, do.

As every girl knows, it is possible to gaze at your reflection in the mirror for a very long time. But simply looking will never change anything about us.

When we look in the mirror of God's word, if we want it to impact our lives we must respond to what we see and then do something about it.

James 1 says,

> '...But the man who looks intently into the perfect law that gives freedom, and continues to do this, not forgetting what he has heard but doing it...'[18]

Not only should our look into God's mirror be done intently, (that means closely, purposefully, keenly, with intent), we must *continue* to stay in God's word. Not just a one-off read every now and again, but a sustained lifestyle of reading and learning what the word of God says about us. If you want to find your identity, your worth and your true value as laid out in the word, then you need to put the effort in and read it, because that's how you'll begin to know.

---

[18] James 1:25 NIV

Knowing God's word is crucial, because unless we know what it says how can we ever know what to believe? Sadly, we are not born with a scholarly knowledge of the word of God already embedded in our hearts. We are required to learn it, to read it and to listen to it. Everyone learns in different ways, so try and find out the best way for you.

If you struggle to remember what you've read you could try writing out key scriptures, memorizing them, speaking them out or putting them around your car, your kitchen, or on your fridge door. Do whatever helps you personally to know the word. Reading it out loud can also be helpful as there is something very powerful about speaking the truth of God's word over yourself.

Or you can buy it on CD and listen to it being read. Find as many creative ways as you can of saturating your life with God's truth.

Soak it up

Just touching the word is not enough; absorbing it is what matters. If I were to spill a glass of water, I could choose to mop it up with a paper towel or with a newspaper. Mopping it up with a newspaper would mean that the paper would get wet, but very little would be absorbed and most would just roll off the page back onto the floor. However, if I used a paper towel, it would completely absorb the water. That's how we need to be with the word of God.

Many people put much effort into knowing the word but then they neglect to listen for his voice. In John 10:27, Jesus said, "My sheep hear my voice…".

The Bible is God's love letter to the world and the more you read it, the more you will grow to love it and hear his voice through it.

Without God's word, it is difficult to learn to hear his voice, but without knowing his voice, the Bible is just a book. It is through a relationship with the Holy Spirit that the Bible is revealed as more than the ancient words of an unseen God. It becomes a clear and consistent message of God's love for his people and for living life his way in freedom and relationship with him.

Changing the software

You can read the word, listen to it, go to theological college, write books about it, but if you don't believe what the word says, then you will never see the true reflection it can show you. James 1:6 says,

> *'You must believe and not doubt, because he who doubts is like a wave of the sea, blown and tossed by the wind…you will be unstable in all you do.'*

As we are reading, hearing and speaking the word, there is a key aspect that must be in play if we are ever going to be free from the old, distorted reflections; we must choose to believe it.

Believing what the word says is fundamental to everything written in this book. If you don't believe it, then you will continue to be deceived by the reflections of the other false mirrors offering you a distorted reflection of your identity. You'll become confused, sure of who you are one minute and doubting the next.

Your life will become unstable, and your confidence, sense of worth and value, will be tossed to and fro by the waves of opinion, circumstances, or by your own internal belief system that simply says, "No, this cannot be true".

Our internal belief system is shaped by our childhood, environment, socio-economic background, and by experiences, circumstances and consequences of choices outside of our control.

For many of us this internal wiring is faulty and sets us up for failure. Our belief system leads us to believe the false reflections of the mirrors described in this book.

Believing is a choice and it's a choice only you can make. Your vicar, pastor, friend, youth leader or family can talk about how much God loves you and what the Bible says about your identity. But if there's something in you that doesn't accept or believe the truth, you will filter their words without taking in the truth contained in them and your internal belief system will remain unchanged.

Unless you make a conscious decision to believe what God says through his word, unless you choose to believe the mirror image he shows you, you will be trapped in a world of unbelief and nothing will change.

MMUK graduate Amy said this at her graduation:

> 'Once God had stripped me of every fake thing that I had previously depended upon, he led me on a journey towards total trust, reliance and dependence on him – my solid foundation. *As I began to dare to believe* that He truly loved me, I found myself able to love myself and thus trust myself to love others without fearing rejection.
>
> I have become secure in my value and learnt that my worth is in Christ alone and that even if everything else turns against me, God will always be with me, rooting for me 100%. Not only is he my solid ground, he is my hope, my joy, my peace, my

> comfort, my light and my Saviour. The lies I had previously built my life upon were weak and temporary, *but the truth of God's Word is unshakeable and it is on this that I now stand, because I believe."*

Amy's sense of identity, worth and value came into line with what God said about her when she chose to believe him.

Faith to step out

In the movie *Indiana Jones and the Last Crusade*, Indiana is involved in a search for the Holy Grail, the cup from which Christ drank at the Last Supper. As the film reaches its climax, Indy must go through three tests in order to reach it.

After overcoming the first two obstacles, the final test requires Indy to step out in faith. He stands at the edge of a wide chasm with no visible way across the divide and yet the book his father gave him tells him to step out and believe.

His adversary says, "It's time to ask yourself what you believe." And as Indy stands facing the vast chasm before him, he has a choice to make. Will he follow the instructions from his father's book and place his faith in what it instructs him to do, or will he base his belief on what he can see with his natural eyes?

In the next room, his father whispers over and over, 'You must believe boy, you must believe...'

As Indy takes a deep breath and makes a choice within himself to trust his father, he steps into the void. And to his amazement, his foot comes down on solid ground! A bridge appears across the chasm that had been there all along but was hidden from Indy's view.

Every time we look in the mirror of God's word and are presented with a true reflection of who we are, we have a choice to make. Believe what it says and act accordingly, or walk away and forget it.

The choice is not a difficult one but so often we complicate it with thoughts and feelings and fears. In the end, it is all about choosing who and what we believe. Deuteronomy 30[19] says,

> *This commandment that I'm commanding you today isn't too much for you, it's not out of your reach. It's not on a high mountain - you don't have to get mountaineers to climb the peak and bring it down to your level and explain it before you can live it. And it's not across the ocean - you don't have to send sailors out to get it, bring it back, and then explain it before you can live it. No. The word is right here and now - as near as the tongue in your mouth, as near as the heart in your chest. Just do it!*

The commandment God gave the Israelites was to choose life, to live believing his word and to act according to it. It is still the same for us today. Will you believe the mirror of his word? Will you choose to continue looking in it and to apply what you read to your everyday life? If you do, you will begin to see the true reflection of who you are. Your confidence will become firmly rooted in him and the foundations of your life become strong.

There is immense power and freedom in choosing to believe God's word about our identity. I believe it's one of the reasons there is such an attack on the self-esteem, confidence and sense of worth of so many women. The enemy knows that if we believe our true reflection in God's mirror, we will become an unstoppable force to be reckoned with and our world will change.

---

[19] Deuteronomy 30:11-14 The Message

Summary: How to use the Compact Mirror of God's word

1. Make the word of God an essential 'accessory' in your daily life, don't just grab it for emergencies, but carry it inside you everywhere you go.

2. Remember that you have to read, learn, and listen to God's word in order to know what to believe. Investing in a relationship requires action. Try sticking post-its on your wall, by your bathroom mirror, or listening to teaching CDs while doing the ironing or driving to work; anything that will immerse you in the truth.

3. Remember to regularly check your reflection in the compact mirror of his word. It's not a once-off glance.

4. Make a choice to believe what God says about your reflection and act like you believe it.

Prayer:

God, thank you that you have made it easy for us to access you. Thank you that we have the freedom to open our Bibles or pray at any time throughout the day.

Help me to make opening the 'compact mirror' of your word a regular practice. Let your living word change my thoughts and actions.

I ask you to make every part of me whole. Give me a passion for reading and absorbing your word. Holy Spirit, help me to hear your voice in everything I do, that I would choose to walk in line with the truth.

As I read the Bible and walk with you, I commit to work in partnership with you to break down any faulty internal belief systems from my past and create new software.

Today, I choose to believe that in you, I am a force to be reckoned with and that I am changing the course of my future and of the people attached to my life for your glory.

In Jesus' name,

Amen.

Chapter 7

Becoming the Mirror

There once was a group of women doing a Bible study on the book of Malachi. As they were studying chapter three they came across verse three which says, 'He will sit as a refiner and purifier of silver.' This verse puzzled the women and they wondered what this meant.

One of the women offered to find out about the process of refining silver and report back to the group. She was so intrigued by the verse that she made an appointment to watch a silversmith at work. She didn't mention anything to him about the reason for her interest beyond her curiosity about the process of refining silver. As she watched the silversmith, he held a piece of silver over the fire and let it heat up. He explained that when refining silver, you have to hold the silver in the middle of the fire where the flames were hottest to burn away all the impurities.

She asked the silversmith if it was true that he had to sit in front of the fire while the silver was being refined. The man answered that yes, he had to sit there holding the silver and he had to keep his eyes on the silver the entire time it was in the fire. For if the silver was left for just a moment too long in the flames, it would be destroyed.

The woman was silent for a moment. Then she asked, 'How do you know when the silver is fully refined?' He smiled at her and answered, Oh, that's the easy part - it's when I see my image reflected in it.

When we stop looking in false mirrors; when we start believing the reflection God's mirror shows us, we will begin to reflect his glory. Our lives become a mirror that shows others who he is. 2 Corinthians 3[20] puts it like this:

> *And we, who with unveiled faces all reflect the Lord's glory, are being transformed into his likeness with ever increasing glory, which comes from the Lord.*

The great work that God does inside of us is about more than us living a good Christian life and becoming nice, well balanced people. It's not just about us. There is a world out there full of brokenness, pain and people who do not know their creator. Ultimately, when we break away from the distorted mirror reflections described in this book and learn to look into the mirror of his word, we become a people who are able to reflect all he is to those around us.

Extraordinarily ordinary

Over the years, I've seen how some people have gone through terrible traumas yet still proclaimed God's truth. God has responded by using their lives to touch others in a powerful way. They have allowed God to turn their mess into a message and their stories inspire thousands to overcome all obstacles and rise above the hardship to bring glory to God.

Yet I have also seen how God has used those who have no great story of dramatic rescue but who have discovered their identity, worth and value in him amidst the quietness of an ordinary looking life.

God will use the broken, the lonely, the abused, the disenfranchised or the whole, the happy and the content.

---

[20] 2 Corinthians 3:18 NIV

He uses whoever makes themselves available to him.   He changes each of us, moulds and shapes us, heals the hurts and in his hands we become more than we could ever dream of.

Don't ever disqualify yourself for any reason - neither the shame of your past nor the favour of your past are reasons not to enter into the purpose God has placed on your life.

A mirror has no choice but to reflect what is in front of it. The mirror of his word reflects anyone who chooses to place themselves in front of it, regardless of their circumstance or background.

It's one of the great joys of my life to watch as broken and distorted reflections find their real mirror image in the face of our God as he transforms the lives of the young women at Mercy Ministries. What excites me even more is when those same young women, once so broken and trapped, go on to transform others in their communities through the power of their true reflection.

I don't know what heroes look like to you but the girls whose stories you are about to read are some of mine…

Sindy's Story

I grew up in a good Christian home in the East part of Germany. But somehow I never felt the love and affection of my father, so my search for love and acceptance began in primary school until I was molested by older boys.

It was about the same time that I got introduced to porn. I found magazines hidden under some bathroom towels and I saw my first hardcore porn movie at a friends' house while her single mom was absent. It shook my world, yet led me into a dependency on pornography.

Comparing myself to the women I saw in the magazines or movies made me feel fat, ugly and stupid. I even prayed to God to make me more attractive so I would be loved.

As I grew older I realized that I started to receive a lot of attention for my looks and body. One of the men I knew recognized my talent for the sex industry & encouraged me to table dance in clubs.

Finally when I couldn't stand living with my parents anymore, or to pretend to be a sweet girl in church which I had to attend, I moved to the US after I finished my A-levels.

I moved to Long Island, but NYC is not the best place to turn an already messed-up young life around.

My desire was to become a Playboy bunny and a famous porn actress. But my plan to make it big in the adult industry got stopped by the painful experiences of abuse along the way.

I knew my life was out of control. I didn't know who I was or what I was supposed to do, so finally I went back to Germany to study at University. But after I got raped in the dorm rooms, I never went back again.

I hit rock bottom and just existed. I felt paralysed and couldn't leave my bed for weeks. That's when I began to pray to God to rescue me.

I remembered a Christian magazine while going to church where I had read a story about an Ex-Porn Actress called Shelley Lubben who had turned to Christ.

I found Shelley Lubben's story on the internet and cried so much while reading her testimony. So I wrote her an e-mail and then we talked over the phone. Shelley told me that I need God, Jesus and the Holy Spirit. But I didn't know where to start, what to do... I just knew... I needed to stop this kind of life otherwise I would die from the inside out.

I became a Christian on the 3 November 2006. I wanted a brand new life and for the first time I felt that it could be possible. Somebody paid for me to go a conference where I heard about Mercy Ministries and I knew I needed to go there, so I could receive help to overcome the issues of my past.

On the 1 October 2008 I walked through the doors of Mercy Ministries UK.

During my time at Mercy, so many chains were broken. I was taught fantastic tools that I still use now in my everyday life. Christ's unconditional love was poured out to me and I began to learn about my identity in Christ.

The name I bore 'Sindy', had haunted me all my life. The name 'Sinful-Sindy' is what I had been called – it had become my identity. 'Sindy – made for sinful things,' the enemy had whispered on many occasions into my heart.

At Mercy I cried out to God: 'Give me a new name – I don't want to be called SIN anymore!'

And God answered gently to me: 'You never have been called Sin, Sindy! SINDY contains two more letters: DY-DIE - Sin has died through your salvation – Sindy, you are called FREEDOM!'

I completely broke down after that revelation from God himself. My sinful past had no power over me anymore.

God is still walking me through the hurts and consequences of the past and shows me how to live life differently. He teaches me through his word, other peoples' testimonies and through lessons learnt myself with the assistance of the Holy Spirit.

I now work in fulltime ministry in Berlin, reaching out to lost girls in the Red Light District. We take them into our accommodation to help them off drugs and alcohol and teach them how to live life with Jesus.

Today I get invited to speak at conferences and seminars on how Jesus has set me free and how to deal with the issues that I struggled with. I am currently developing a Self Help and Recovery Group for (Ex-) Sex & Porn Addicts in co-operation with an Austrian based ministry.
I also got the opportunity to teach the girls at Mercy Ministries UK spending three days with them. It made me be so thankful for what Jesus has done for me through that wonderful place and precious staff!'

Kirsten's Story

For much of my life, I lived in a counterfeit reality; a reality pinned together by one essential lie; I could never change, and it held me captive for years.

I grew up in a Christian home. My dad was a local pastor. However, what I experienced at home did not reflect the truth of who God was. My dad sat with unhealed wounds, which manifested in anger and addictions. I never felt safe and was always on my best behaviour, lest I anger him. As both my father and my pastor, my dad reflected a distorted image of who God is. This God, I decided, I wanted nothing to do with.

By the time I was eleven, life at home was getting worse. My mum, concerned about the well-being of her children, made the difficult decision to leave my dad. From that point on I saw very little of him. I loved my dad deeply but, the truth is, life was easier without him and I was relieved. Then, a year later, he died and guilt overwhelmed me for ever wanting him gone. 'I'm a terrible person!' I thought.

It was only one of many lies that increasingly stormed my mind. 'You're no good', 'worthless', 'fat' and 'ugly' – I believed them all! Dwelling on them day and night, I constantly compared myself to others and in my mind I simply did not measure up. I strived for perfection; to gain approval and acceptance.

I worked hard at school; I dieted, I exercised, determined to look like that girl I thought I ought to be. Failing that, I sought solace in alcohol, drugs and the wrong kind of love, trying to escape my painful reality. I hoped that somehow things would be different when I sobered up. But mostly, they were worse.

Yet throughout it all, I could not shake the feeling that God was not too far away. Having surrendered my life to Him as a child, something inside told me He was the answer to the constant ache in my heart. Still, for years I ignored His outstretched hand, stumbling along, doing it my way. I fought Him at every turn, but the more I struggled, the tighter He seemed to hold on.

By the time I walked through the doors of Mercy Ministries UK, I was a shadow of the person God created me to be. Only six months later I left transformed. Armed with the truth of God's word and my head held high, I was well on my way to becoming the person He always knew I was.

I learned that most of my life I had been living a false reality, built upon lies. But most amazing of all, I learned I had the power to change! Taking one lie at a time I broke its hold over my life, replacing it with God's truth and His thoughts towards me. It was not easy, it took time and I had to make the choice to daily stand and fight: a choice I still make today, and will continue to make tomorrow.

Now each day is one of discovery. Each day I take another step forward, becoming more and more the person God created me to be. Before I was born He placed in me a desire to write. That desire took me to South Africa, where I have just finished writing the stories of eight Zulu women who live in an informal settlement, in the suburbs of Durban.

And while their culture and background are vastly different from mine, I have discovered we all experience the same pain in our hearts. So, drawing on the experiences from my own life, I found words to give voice to theirs.

Now I know, in God's hands nothing is wasted. If we let Him, He will heal our hearts and He will take the pain of our past and use it for good, bringing glory to His name!

Hannah's story

I walked through the doors of Mercy Ministries UK a broken, lost and very insecure 18 year old. The real me had become buried so deep that I'd find myself looking in the mirror and many times it would almost be as if it was an unknown face staring back. I had two lives, with two very different audiences. Years of experience had taught me how to keep one life very hidden.

Looking in from the outside I had the perfect family; the perfect life and unless I chose to let you in, you wouldn't know there was anything wrong.

But I'd lost who the real Hannah was, I wasn't even sure that she still existed and even if she did still exist, I had absolutely no idea how to go about getting her back.

Early teenage years had taught me not to trust men - it didn't matter who they were and it didn't matter how well I knew them, because life's experiences had taught me that the world wasn't a safe place. So I developed a response within me of: 'well if danger is eventually going to find me I'd rather find it first!'

Good time party girl consumed one life, whilst going to church on a Sunday masked the other. Regular cocaine use, excessive exercise and diet pills quickly became my best friend, fashion magazines became my biggest enemy and striving to be thin became my goal.

I'd allowed life's experiences to mar me, to place its stamp of worth on me. Involved in a manipulative relationship, trapped in a cycle of addiction, all this had become normal life. This life was spiraling out of control, whilst the other I was clinging to only by my fingertips. Both worlds eventually collided full force.

Mercy loved me through a time of brokenness. They took me as I was, met me where I was at and they helped show me that there's never a 'too late with God.' This one thing I know - God specialises in the broken, he's the master at taking something so broken, so damaged and so hurting and he's the artist who turns it into something so beautiful; he willingly does that exchange.

He simply loves us and that's it. He doesn't love us by the standards of what Hello or OK magazine say love to be, but he loves us with the love that a King says it is to be for his Princesses!

Life since Mercy has been awesome, with their help the foundations in my life that were once shattered and so disintegrated, have now become solid and secure foundations that cannot be shaken and because of that, new layers have now been built on top.

After I graduated from Mercy Ministries UK, I joined an organization called Watoto and spent a year on a missions trip serving in Gulu, Uganda, where I worked with some of the world's most beautiful babies. I also worked with AIDS victims, the malnourished, ex-child soldiers and many broken, hurting, rape victims.

After arriving back home, I began an internship for a year working for Mercy Ministries UK on the Development Team. It was such a privilege to see behind the scenes and be part of helping other young women struggling with issues like I once was.

The very thing I vowed I'd never allow myself to feel again, that word I so deeply feared, the very word that broke me, is in fact the very journey God has been taking me on and using me for.

To show his love, an unconditional love, a never failing love to a hurting and broken generation and showing them that there's 'a never a too late' is one of the greatest joys of my life…'

Grace's Story.

'Mine really is a story of Grace. There have been many times in my life that I felt like either I couldn't go on and I would end it or circumstances out of my control would end my life. I placed value on what people said to me and thought of me so my life became completely trapped by lies and by the need to have people's approval.

I believed that I was fat, ugly, useless and before long these lies turned into bigger and bigger lies which consumed my mind. According to my own beliefs about myself, I was mad, evil and nothing better than a prostitute. When I looked in the mirror I saw obesity, so I over-exercised and under-ate.

I had a drink problem that I managed to hide from my family, which covered up all the repressed feelings of anger, pain and bitterness. I would do impulsive destructive acts, like try to jump out of moving vehicles, I had no fear of that, and yet I was trapped in the fear of the everyday usual routine of being me.

I kept these beliefs about myself hidden inside me, so to everyone on the outside I seemed happy and very capable. I had got away with fooling people for a long time until I couldn't go on any longer.

I came into Mercy not really knowing what way was up. Having been brought up in a Christian home I thought I knew everything about God. I thought I was helpless because 'the best stuff in the world' – Jesus Christ and the Bible - 'hadn't worked before'.

But what I realised at Mercy was that though I knew lots *about* God, I didn't *know* God. I was surrounded by strong women of God who day by day operated in love and in their true identity in Christ. They knew who they were and were proud of it; I was just proud and didn't know who I was! I began a journey of getting to know God for myself and gradually I began to see myself as he sees me.

I was released from the lies that had haunted me for so long as each time I began to choose to believe God's word instead of people's words.

After I graduated I served for a year in my local church and learnt how to serve God and the value of a servant hearted people. Then I went on a year long missions trip to Africa to work with orphans and women. Now that I am back in England, I am proud to say I am the first UK graduate to be on staff at Mercy Ministries UK. What a privilege it is to be on the other side and be able to be a reflection of God to those who are facing some of the very same fears, lies and behaviours I once faced and am now free from.'

To reflect his glory...

I include these stories to give you hope, to encourage and inspire you to become all that God has called you to be. I pray that you will know that no matter what your past looks like; good, bad or ugly- your future is one of hope, of purpose and of destiny.

This hope and this future is not just for our own benefit - let's not become so engrossed in our own journey, by our own need to find a true reflection that we lose sight of those whose reflections are not only distorted but completely shattered.

Let's keep pressing into God, let's keep finding our identity, security and value in who he says we are, because when that happens in our lives- when we start living in the truth of his true mirror image of us, then we become those who can reflect the glory of his face and .so help others break free from false reflections.

Appendix I

False reflections versus God's truth

False reflection - I am unlovable and unworthy. If you knew the real me, you would reject me. No one really likes me.

God's truth - With God's help, I will learn to be myself and trust him to bring people into my life that will appreciate me and respect me for who I am. My worth is in who God says I am.

But the very hairs on your head are numbered. Do not fear therefore; you are of more value than many sparrows.
Luke 12:7

God made him who had no sin (Jesus) to be sin for us, so that in him we might become the righteousness of God.
2 Corinthians 5:21

To the praise of his glorious grace, which he has freely given us in the one he loves. In him we have redemption through his blood, the forgiveness of sins, in accordance with the riches of God's grace.
Ephesians 1:6-7

False reflection - Even when I do my best, it is not good enough. I can never meet the standard.

God's truth - I am fully loved, completely accepted, and totally pleasing to God. Regardless of how much I do or fail to do, I will remain fully loved, completely accepted, and totally pleasing to God. I choose to surrender to him, trusting my faith in him and his ability to sustain me. I will seek to be a God pleaser, not a people pleaser.

If the Lord delights in a man's way, he makes his steps firm; although he stumble, he will not fall, for the Lord upholds him with his hand.
Psalm 37:23-24.

I can do all things through Christ who strengthens me.
Philippians 4:13

But seek first his kingdom and his righteousness, and all these things will be given to you as well.
Matthew 6:33

False reflection - I will always be insecure and fearful. I am a bad person.

God's truth - I can be confident in him who created me. I will draw my security, courage, and identity from what God says about me.

For God did not give us a spirit of timidity, but a spirit of power, of love and of self-discipline.
2 Timothy 1:7

You, dear children, are from God and have overcome them, because the one who is in you is greater than the one who is in the world.
1 John 4:4

There is no fear in love. But perfect love drives out fear, because fear has to do with punishment. The one who fears is not made perfect in love.
1 John 4:18

Be strong and courageous. Do not be terrified; do not be discouraged, for the Lord your God is with you wherever you go.
Joshua 1:8-9

False reflection - I always make wrong decisions. I am unable to take care of myself or make wise decisions. I am out there all alone.

God's truth - I choose to believe that God will help me to make wise decisions as I ask him for direction for my life. If I align my decisions with the word of God, I will consistently make the right choice. God will protect me and keep me.

If any of you lacks wisdom, he should ask God, who gives generously to all without finding fault, and it will be given to him.
James 1:5

Call to me and I will answer you and tell you great and unsearchable things you do not know.
Jeremiah 33:3

Your word is a lamp for my feet and a light for my path.
Psalm 119:105
Trust in the Lord with all your heart and lean not on your own understanding; in all your ways acknowledge him, and

he will make your paths straight.
Psalm 3:5-6

If you remain in me and my words remain in you, ask whatever you wish, and it will be given you.
John 15:7

False reflection - I will always be lonely.

God's truth - God says he sets the solitary in families. I choose to believe that he will see to it that I will always belong to a family and have friends if I show myself to be friendly.

God sets the lonely in families, he leads forth the prisoners with singing; but the rebellious live in a sun-scorched land.
Psalm 68:6

A man who has friends must himself be friendly, but there is a friend who sticks closer than a brother.
Psalm 18:24

Delight yourself in the Lord and he will give you the desires of your heart. Commit your way to the Lord; trust in him and he will do this.
Psalm 37:4-5

About the Author

Arianna Walker is a wife and a mother, she is a friend, a daughter, a sister, as well as a leader, speaker and author…and therein lies the ultimate challenge of her life-giving her all to everything. Hers is a story of an ordinary kind of person, living an ordinary kind of life yet serving an extraordinary God. She is passionate about activating a sense of purpose and destiny in the hearts and minds of those who would otherwise have disqualified themselves from being used by God.

Arianna is the Executive Director of Mercy Ministries UK and has been intricately involved in the development of Mercy Ministries in the UK since its earliest beginnings in 1999. Her younger sister, Debbie, became the first girl from the UK to graduate the Mercy programme in America years before Mercy Ministries UK existed. Seeing Debbie's life utterly transformed became a catalyst for Arianna's continued fervour and passion to see the work of Mercy Ministries established in the UK. Now, 10 years since her sister's graduation, Arianna has the pleasure of leading the MMUK team, which includes her sister Debbie as Programme Director.

The home based in West Yorkshire represents the beginning of Mercy Ministries' journey in the UK. Since opening its doors in 2006, more than a hundred girls have had an opportunity to experience God's unconditional love, forgiveness and life transforming power through the residential programme and countless more through conferences, speaking engagements and events where Mercy Ministries has been represented. With an extension completed in 2011 to increase the intake from 10 beds to 22 and more homes planned across the country, Arianna and her team remain focused on continuing to make a difference to broken lives in the UK and Europe in partnership with local churches across the nation.

If you would like to know more about the work of Mercy Ministries UK, if would like to apply to the programme or if you would like to invite Arianna or one of the team to speak at your conference, event or church, please contact Mercy Ministries UK at: info@mercyministries.co.uk or check out the website: www.mercyministries.co.uk

About Mercy Ministries

Mercy Ministries was founded in America in 1983 by Nancy Alcorn. It exists to provide opportunities for young women to experience God's unconditional love, forgiveness and life transforming power in partnership with local churches.

Mercy Ministries provide a six-month residential Christian discipleship programme for young women aged 18-28 suffering from life controlling issues, such as eating disorders, self-harm, depression, and the effects of abuse in all its forms.

There are three founding principles by which Mercy Ministries operates worldwide:

1. We do not charge for any part of the programme or accommodation

2. We tithe 10% of all our unrestricted donations to other Christian charities, ministries or churches

3. We do not take any Government or other funding that would hinder us from delivering a Christ centred programme

We address all aspects of a young woman's well being - physical, spiritual and emotional - and deal with the root causes of her issues, rather than merely medicating the symptoms.

The programme consists of:

- A discipleship programme called *Choices that Bring Change,* which offers in-depth individualised sessions on a one to one basis
- Biblical teaching
- Life skills training
- Fitness and nutrition
- Residential care 24 hours a day, 7 days a week
- Recreation
- Resources

If you would like more information on the work of Mercy Ministries UK or if you would like to apply to the programme, please visit www.mercyministries.co.uk or contact Mercy Ministries UK, Cragg Royd, Lowertown, Oxenhope, Keighley, West Yorkshire, BD22 9JE